How Do Humans Become Moral?

Social Domain Approach to Moral Development

Jeong Yeon Hwang, S.J.

First Edition

Hwang, Jeong Yeon

How do humans become moral?

Social domain approach to moral development

Includes bibliographical references and index.

ISBN13: 9798744195748

Preface

After I taught the course on moral development for five years at the Institute of Psychology at the Pontifical Gregorian University, I had a desire to write a book to help university students understand the theories of moral development. As there are good books at the level of introduction, I found that students would understand the outlines of the principal theories of moral development such as the theories of Piaget and Kohlberg and also the explicit ideas of the founders of important psychological approaches on morality such as Freud and Skinner. However, many students did not easily comprehend the continuities and discontinuities between different theories on this issue. I think that this difficulty on the part of students is related to their limited grasp of the basic viewpoints of these scholars on human nature, social relationships, and morals. Thus, I want to help them to reflect on the perspectives and premises of the various theories of moral development (e.g., psychoanalysis, behaviorism, cognitive theory, evolutionary psychology, sociobiology) and recognize the common foundations and diverging ideas in the theories of Piaget, Kohlberg, and Turiel.

In this book, the theoretical frame of Piaget (1932, 1950) will provide me with a cognitive developmental perspective for my reviews and discussions. His theories on moral and cognitive development help me to identify and integrate various characteristics and changes in the developmental processes of moral judgments. With the cognitive developmental perspective based on his ideas, I have no intention of excluding the role of emotions in moral judgment. Rather, I view the relationship between cognition and emotion as inseparable and irreplaceable (Piaget, 1954). Human rationality cannot function without emotional resources and vice versa. In a real-life situation, it is not plausible fully to understand the moral judgments of individuals by attending only to one of them. Without creating any global discrepancy between them, thus, I would like to review various studies on the question of how children grow in moral reasoning. Moreover, the cognitive developmental perspective does not follow any dichotomous views on the relationship between organism and environment, which may regard one of the two as a main source of development. Instead, it denotes that children and adolescents engage in interactions with social environments including other humans, institutions, and legal systems. Through the interactions, they develop their capacities to reflect on the implications of incidents in their social life, formulate moral conceptions such as fairness and rights, and apply them to their decision-making processes. Because no one can become moral in a vacuum and no environmental forces totally regulate the moral reasoning of humans, it is essential to maintain my focus on the reciprocal relations between individual and environment in the study of moral development. In the end, as it is a developmental perspective, it seeks to figure out the similarities and differences between children and adolescents in moral judgments. I am also interested in differences between young and old adolescents. As Piaget and Kohlberg did not specify developmental changes in this period, I would like to review what has been found regarding the variations in moral reasoning during adolescence. Moreover, I aim at explicating developmental trajectories in the reasoning of children and adolescents by focusing on the interactions between various cognitive and emotional aspects in their judgments.

Quite a few colleagues in the fields of philosophy and theology asked me what came after the stage theory of Kohlberg (1969, 1971). To them, I usually made two points. First, I explained that the social domain theory of Turiel (1983, 2002) has contributed much to the development of this field after Kohlberg. Secondly, I wanted to say that the research of Piaget (1932) on the moral judgments of children preceded that of Kohlberg. Certainly, the influence of Kohlberg on our understanding of moral development is immense and substantial. His philosophical clarifications and empirical endeavors made for remarkable progress in the studies of moral development. This huge impact might make others feel that no one is there before or after him. However, his theory did not appear out of nowhere but originated from the studies of Piaget. After the stage theory of Kohlberg, the studies of moral development based on the social domain theory of Turiel have brought in many significant findings such as the early emergence of moral judgments among young children and the non-linear developmental changes in adolescence. Therefore, I focus on the theoretical and practical implications of the transition from the two stages of moral development of Piaget to the three levels (and six stages) of Kohlberg and the evolution from the stage theory of Kohlberg to the domain theory of Turiel. As Turiel (1983) found the children's capacity to distinguish morality from convention at an early age, his social domain approach reveals a new possibility to view the development of moral reasoning along with its relationship to non-moral reasoning.

This book consists of six chapters whose titles are in the form of questions. 1. Are humans born with morals? 2. Does evolution make humans moral? 3. Is emotion more important than reasoning in moral judgments? 4. Do children differentiate morality from convention? 5. Does freedom help children become moral? 6. Do children consider the multifaceted aspects of an event? In the first three chapters, I deal with some questions to find a right approach to moral development. More specifically, I discuss the presence of innate morals, the influence of evolution, and the relationship between emotion and cognition. These themes help me to explain how to view humans, development, the interaction between organism and environment, and the relationship between cognition and emotion. Then, I explain the social domain approach of Turiel to moral development in the other three chapters. I discuss the implications of the distinction between morality and convention, the relationship between freedom and morality, and the coordination of the domains of social reasoning. It is worthwhile to explore what researchers with this approach have found in the studies of moral judgments with children and adolescents across cultures for those who consider morality to be a precious issue in this world.

I would like to mention that this book can be helpful to any students and teachers in the fields of psychology, education, philosophy, and theology who have studied the introductory level of moral development in psychology. Above all, I found that the theories of Piaget, Kohlberg, and Turiel are not easy for many university students to comprehend especially when they read their original writings. The students need some background knowledge and theoretical frames to understand the pioneering studies of these scholars. Basically, moral development is a profound and multifaceted theme. There is no single theory which reveals the whole truth of human morality. Thus, it is essential to analyze comparatively the varied ideas on this issue from a balanced perspective. I will try to review diverse ideas and experiments on moral development and help readers develop a scientific perspective to evaluate the works of different approaches to the moral reasoning of humans. Hopefully, this book can become a bridge between the introductory books of psychology and the original works of important thinkers and researchers on the issues of moral development.

Lastly, I would like to thank Fr. Franco Imoda, S.J., Fr. Timothy Healy, S.J., Fr. James Corkery, S.J., and Fr. Lancy Dias, S.J. for reading the manuscript for my book, correcting writing errors, and suggesting some points to reconsider.

Jeong Yeon Hwang, S.J.

International College of Gesù, Rome

Table of Contents

1

Are Humans Born with Morals?

The good disposition of human nature is like water's tendency to flow down. There are no men who are not innately good, just as there is no water that does not flow down. Now, by splashing you can make water leap up higher than your forehead, and by churning it you can make it flow up a hill, but how could this be the nature of water? It is merely a result of force. The fact that men can be made to act badly merely shows that human nature is like this as well. (Mencius, 6A. 1, as translated in Eno, 2016).

As one of the most influential ancient Chinese philosophers and sages, Mencius (孟子, 372-289 BC) maintained, humans possess innate moral dispositions. Many others challenged his ideas on human nature. Especially, Xunzi (荀子, 313-238 BC) was known to criticize Mencius by arguing that humans are originally bad (Chong, 2008; Feng, 1975).

Discussions and arguments about the inborn morals of human beings may be found in the East as well as the West and in the past as well as the present. Not only ancient eastern philosophers, but also quite a few contemporary western psychologists discuss eagerly the issue of innate morals. For instance, Bloom and Wynn (2016) in the U.S. believe that humans are born with certain moral capacities and argue against those psychologists and philosophers who suggest that infants are not moral. Reflecting on the long history and ubiquity of the controversy on the innate morals of humans, it would be informative to evaluate and analyze diverse ideas and approaches to the question "Are humans born with morals?" in order to facilitate scientific studies of moral development in a constructive manner.

In this chapter, I will review the debates and analyses about human innate moral dispositions. With this review, I do not intend to say "yes" or "no" to the question of whether humans are born with morals but I hope to suggest a valid way to analyze the theories and experiments on this issue. The inundation of new findings, as a characteristic of the contemporary scientific world, seems to be true for the studies on moral development. However, it is uncertain whether the large number of empirical results substantially helps our understanding of the morals of children. I think that a simple description of the ideas and findings of researchers can hardly make a difference in our understanding of human morality. It is, therefore, necessary to fathom the inner world of these researchers and evaluate how solid and logical their studies are. With this idea, I will try to evaluate the underlying thoughts and perspectives of scholars on this issue and discuss what point of view needs to be adopted in the studies of innate morals.

First, I will introduce the debate between Mencius and Xunzi on human nature in order to find some guidelines for the studies of innate morals. This old debate can teach contemporary psychologists how crucial it is to define basic concepts appropriately and to take a developmental perspective on the issue of innate morals in a meaningful academic inquiry. Secondly, I will analyze the classification of Hoffman (1970) on the ideas of Freud, Piaget, and Skinner on the moral dispositions of infants. I would like to discuss the authenticity of this classification by reviewing the original writings of the three classical scholars. Thirdly, I will introduce contemporary studies of human nature in the field of developmental psychology. Quite a few have conducted experiments with infants to know how early they can discern between moral and immoral behaviors. I want to review how they interpret the results of their studies with children and figure out if their studies are based on a developmental perspective. Lastly, I will explain how significant it is to interpret the behaviors of children from children's own point of view.

Chapter One

Mencius and Xunzi: The Ancient Debate of Goodness vs. Badness

A question about the innate morality of humans reveals its complex nature in the famous debate about human morality between Mencius and Xunzi in ancient China. This antique debate may demonstrate some important issues of contemporary arguments on the question of innate morals. Basically, these two great philosophers showed two contrasting ideas about human nature. Mencius developed the theory of the original goodness of human nature (*xìngshànshuō* 性善說), whereas Xunzi, that of the original evil (*xìng'èshuō* 性惡說). Both of them constructed their theories in a logical manner by proposing their premises and confronting some possible objections to their theories at the same time.

Mencius: The Innate Goodness of Humans

In the text of Mencius, the core of human morality is explained with a thought experiment based on the following narrative.

> Why do I say that all people possess within them a moral sense that cannot bear the suffering of others? Well, imagine now a person who, all of a sudden, sees a small child on the verge of falling down into a well. Any such person would experience a sudden sense of fright and dismay. This feeling would not be something he summoned up in order to establish good relations with the child's parents. He would not purposefully feel this way in order to win the praise of their friends and neighbors. Nor would he feel this way because the screams of the child would be unpleasant. (Mencius, 2A. 6, as translated in Eno, 2016).

This way of argumentation seems to be very similar to contemporary experiments in the field of psychology. In interviews or experiments for psychological studies, a good number of researchers present to the participants of studies a scenario in a form of storytelling, narrative, video, or play, and ask questions of them or observe them with specific inquiries to understand their judgments and behaviors.

Mencius created the scenario of a small child on the verge of falling down a well, which provokes a sense of pity and a desire to rescue the child in the heart of human beings. This particular sentiment is named commiseration or compassion.

After the presentation of the dangerous situation of the child, Mencius asked probing questions in order to verify the authenticity of the internal reactions of observers. His main concern lies in the question of whether personal desires for rewards and benefits motivate the human benevolent reaction to the child in danger. Thus, he tested if the individual who experienced commiseration toward the child felt that way because of his egoistic motives such as expanding his personal relationships, gaining a good reputation, or removing unpleasant stimuli such as the scream of the child. It is obvious that most people would respond negatively to these probing questions. In his ideas, thus, the compassionate human reaction in the narrative is rooted in innate morals. It is purely altruistic and genuinely moral as it is neither regulated by the logic of give-and-take nor motivated by the expectation of rewards following good deeds (see Kohlberg 1969, 1971; Skinner, 1961). While Mencius was confirming that all humans possess innate moral senses such as commiseration, he made a close connection between human nature and dignity. Humans are noble not because of their possessions or education, but because of the innate goodness which every single person has (see Zhang, 2016, pp. 23−24). His ideas become a foundation for the idea of the protection of human dignity in a Chinese culture.

Mencius faced many questions about his theory of human goodness and answered them by explaining the functions and limitations of the innate morals. One of the questions was as follows: "How can human beings do heinous crimes if they have a good nature?" He confronted this question in a number of ways. Above all, he explained the nature of innate moral senses as human potentials to become noble and righteous. According to Mencius, commiseration and other moral senses[1] in every human being should not be viewed as the complete form of morality, but the seeds of morality (Mencius 2A. 6, as translated in Eno, 2016)). As a seed of a tree grows and bears fruits, innate moral senses develop into virtues by interior reflection and ethical cultivation. The feeling of compassion does not automatically induce a virtuous behavior. As the presence of the seed of commiseration does not mean the actualization of the human moral potential or the accomplishment of human morality, Mencius did not exclude a possibility that humans fail to be moral in real social interactions. Notwithstanding the moral failures of people, inborn moral senses do not disappear in their nature and are considered to be a foundation of human civilization.

Mencius did not stop his argument with the verification of human nature but continued with the process of becoming moral. During the course of life, all individuals have both possibilities, i.e., growing noble and righteous or becoming ignorant and corrupt according to the extent of moral development. Mencius also specified the method of moral development by answering the question of what people should do to become moral. They ought to pursue self-cultivation which consists of reflection and practice (Mencius 2A. 2, as translated in Eno, 2016). When they discern between decent and debased motivations, decide to follow noble inspirations, and put them into practice in a repeated manner, the spirit of goodness grows in them and expands into diverse dimensions of life. It is only through this process of self-cultivation that human beings become moral, noble, and righteous. When Mencius' theory of human goodness is understood from a developmental perspective, his intentions become clear and evident. Every single person possesses innate moral senses but becomes moral only through a process of self-cultivation.

---

[1] Along with commiseration, there are three other innate moral senses; shame, respect, and a sense of right and wrong (Eno, 2016).

Xunzi: The Innate Badness of Humans

Contrary to Mencius, Xunzi maintained that human nature is bad. While he did not deny that human beings can behave in a morally sound manner, he argued that they can live this way only by restraining and correcting their evil nature as humans. In other words, radical changes of human nature are necessary for any individual to do good things, since the goodness of humans is not a part of human nature but an acquired value through discipline (Fang, 1981).

Xunzi explained in metaphors how humans become moral despite innate badness.

> ... crooked wood must await steaming and straightening on the shaping frame, and only then does it become straight. Blunt metal must await honing and grinding, and only then does it become sharp. Now since people's nature is bad, they must await its teachers and proper models, and only then do they become correct. (Xunzi, 23, as translated in Hutton, 2014, p. 317)

According to Xunzi, individuals can never become moral by following their nature, since it is disordered and wicked. As human goodness does not have its roots in a human person, the sources of goodness are to be found outside individuals. The main sources of morality are comprised of the educational and corrective systems of society. In order for human babies to grow into morally mature adults, they are supposed to enter into a long and assiduous process of learning principally by adhering to the civil laws and regulations of society and imitating the examples of noble figures.

Then, what can be the human innate potentials which help humans become moral in the theory of Xunzi? It is somewhat puzzling to think about the source of moral development in humans in his theory. Nevertheless, there must be certain non-moral innate qualities responsible for moral growth, as Xunzi believed that humans could become righteous and polite. According to Zhang (2016),

Xunzi saw the intellectual capacity of humans as the foundation of human development, with which humans can change their evil nature and become morally honorable sages. This capacity also includes human efforts to acquire knowledge. Learning does not take place in an automatic manner. Instead, individuals have to work hard to develop their knowledge. Despite their evil nature, there is a hope for moral development because humans have the innate potentials to make deliberate efforts to learn wisdom and virtue, transform their evil nature, and become noble and righteous (see Hutton, 2014, p. 321). The optimal condition of the transformation of human nature can be described as the integration of the innate intellectual capacity and deliberate effort. Due to difficulty in making the effort to study, however, many individuals do not become moral and noble. Only a small number of people become noble sages.

Beyond the Ancient Debate over Human Nature

At this juncture, I would like to pinpoint a couple of complications in the debate between Xunzi and Mencius and suggest some directions for a fruitful discussion about innate morals. First of all, the contrast between the two ancient philosophers is not truly authentic as their comprehensions on the main aspects of human nature are not identical. They clearly revealed a sharp contrast in terms of their understanding of the quality of human nature. Xunzi considered it bad, whereas Mencius, good. However, they demonstrated differences in their ideas about the components of human nature. This disparity creates problems in their debate. Human physical instincts such as eating and resting are the principal aspects of human nature for Xunzi, whereas human emotions such as compassion are the main components of human nature for Mencius. Due to these differences with respect to the concept of human nature in their theories, it is somewhat problematic to consider them genuinely contradictory. By observing this danger of unauthentic discussion due to a lack of common foundation, I would like to maintain that it is crucial to understand correctly the intentions and terminologies of thinkers in order to make the study of human nature logical and scientific. As the debate between Mencius and Xunzi did not start on the shared understanding about the components of human nature, the well-known discrepancy between their theories may not be subjected to a productive scientific analysis.

Secondly, some communal aspects of the two theories are present in their views on moral development. Both Mencius and Xunzi saw human innate qualities as being far from authentic morality and agreed that humans have a capacity to become moral. Mencius believed that humans could cultivate and nourish innate moral seeds. Xunzi also acknowledged the potentials of humans to learn moral norms and discipline their behaviors for the achievement of righteousness and civility (see Goldin, 2018). There are, still, subtle differences between them in terms of the mechanism of moral development. Mencius focused on the natural growth of innate morals through self-cultivation, whereas Xunzi emphasized the role of environment in providing humans with the moral standards to learn and follow. Despite these differences, Xunzi and Mencius did agree on the importance of developmental process without falling into any type of determinism. In ancient China, there were some examples of deterministic ideas on morality. For instance, a philosopher argued that some are born with a good human nature and others with a bad human nature (Feng, 1975). Compared to this example, the theories of Mencius and Xunzi demonstrate the path and method of moral development in a logical and practical manner. As another take-away point from the ancient debate, thus, I would like to suggest that discussions on human nature or innate morals need to be reviewed from a developmental perspective in order to discuss the genuine differences between varying ideas on innate morals and figure out their concrete and practical implications for moral growth.

Freud, Piaget, and Skinner on Innate Morals

One of the classical classifications of various perspectives on human nature in the field of psychology can be found in the writing of Hoffman (1970). As a psychologist, he started his text on moral development, mentioning three philosophical views on human nature.

The three perspectives were named original sin, innate purity, and *tabula rasa* (i.e., blank slate; infants are born without any knowledge). According to this classification, the perspective of psychoanalysis on morality, whose representative figure is Freud, is based on the idea of original sin. Instead, cognitive approaches, whose principal scholar is Piaget, view human nature as innately pure. Lastly, behaviorism or learning theory, whose pioneering scholar is Skinner, was founded on the idea of *tabula rasa*. However, this classification may be based on a subjective impression of the three great psychologists. Thus, I would like to review its validity by examining what they really intended to communicate regarding the innate morality of infants.

Freud: Infants without Superego

Freud (1933, as translated in Strachey, 1974), as the founder of psychoanalysis, viewed the mind of an infant as amoral, i.e., neither moral nor immoral, even though he seemed to suggest a negative image of human nature in his theory.

> Even if conscience is something 'within us', yet it is not so from the first. In this it is a real contrast to sexual life, which is in fact there from the beginning of life and not only a later addition. But, as is well known, young children are amoral and possess no internal inhibitions against their impulses striving for pleasure (Freud, 1933/1974, p. 4671).

According to him, a new born baby is full of id, that is, physiological and biological impulses (Freud, 1923). There is no room for morals in the beginning of life, because conscience, as a mechanism of self-control, is not yet formed in the psyche of neonates. Unlike the understanding of Hoffman (1970), thus, it is quite clear that psychoanalytic perspectives on the innate morals of humans entail the idea of *tabula rasa*, because neither moral contents nor original sins are installed in a built-in manner in the mind of the infant.

Despite a clear remark of Freud about the amoral nature of infants, quite a few understand that his theory is based on the idea of so-called original sin (Hoffman, 1970). This perception may come from the ideas of Freud on human instincts. According to him, human beings possess Eros (i.e., sexual drive) and Death (i.e., aggressive impulse) as two distinctive instincts from the beginning of life (Freud, 1930). As the limitless realization of these instinctual wishes could endanger the safety and wellness of others, human nature seems to be considered evil and sinful from a psychoanalytic perspective. This perception or evaluation of Freud's theory, however, does not correspond to his original understanding of moral development.

Even though infants and toddlers are equipped with socially unacceptable drives and persistently attempt to realize them, they do not have a capacity to evaluate what they pursue and how they behave before the formation of the superego. In other words, there is no internal observer or disciplinarian to identify and control any drives within children between birth and the formation of the superego. Eventually children acquire morality in the process of psychosexual development, and their morality is to be established with the formation of the superego at the phallic stage of psychosexual development (i.e., three to six years of age). (see Freud, 1923, 1930, see Turiel, 1983). Therefore, it is necessary to note that Freud's perspective on morality is developmental, in order not to be guided by a seemingly negative impression about his ideas on the morality of new born babies.

For Freud (1930), the moral development of children takes place mainly in the relationship between children and parents. Through the resolution of the Oedipus complex at the phallic stage, children come to form the superego which consists of ego ideal and conscience (Freud, 1923). On the one hand, the ego ideal of the superego is constructed through children's acceptance of the moral ideals and standards of parents. Children themselves do not construct the norms and ideals, but adults have already prepared them. What children do is to internalize them, that is, to accept the norms and ideals of parents as their own and behave according to them. On the other hand, the conscience of the superego is developed as the controller of the internal thoughts and external behaviors of the ego, reflecting on the norms of the ego ideal. By the function of superego, children began to incorporate the rules and recommendations of parents, instead of competing with them, and activate the conscience as an internal force to monitor and control their behaviors. This function of conscience is crucial for them to become valid and capable members of family, school, and society. This developmental process makes clear the nature of Freud's perspective on morality. Amoral infants grow and become moral to be competent members of society (i.e., socialization) by internalizing the norms and standards of parents and the authority of society (i.e., internalization).

Piaget: Infants without Innate Schema

Piaget did not maintain that neonates are endowed with morals or mention the innate purity of the mind of infants in an ethical sense, unlike the interpretation of Hoffman (1970). Above all, Piaget (1950) thought that morality is part of human knowledge. As new born babies enter into the world without any knowledge about humans and society (Piaget, 1950, 1952, 1965, 1971), there is simply no room in the mind of infants for any innate moral knowledge. As human knowledge cannot be inherited biologically, all humans have to construct their perceptions and thoughts from birth. Like Freud, the mind of children is rather close to the idea of *tabula rasa* in terms of morality in Piaget's theory.

If the amoral nature of infants is described with a Piagetian terminology, it can be said that new born babies start their lives without any innate schema of morality. Piaget (1952) used the concept of schema to refer to a specific content of intelligence in a broad manner. It can be a perceptual schema such as looking or a sensorimotor schema such as sucking reflex. Although these kinds of schemata are not fully intellectual conceptions, they are necessary for the development of symbolic schemata such as language and operational schemata such as conservation.[2] When infants start their human development, they do not have any simple innate schemata but immediately start to construct simple ones. As the living organisms of humans possess the innate functions, which are invariant throughout the course of life, infants with no schema are able to generate various mental structures with these functions along the stages of moral and intellectual development.

The two main innate functions of humans are assimilation and accommodation (see Piaget, 1952; Piaget & Inhelder, 1969). Assimilation refers to human mental activities to incorporate all the given information into one's pre-existing schemata. In this assimilatory process, an infant takes new objects and fits them into its cognitive schemata. For instance, small babies tend to grasp various objects around them and put them into their mouths when they possess schemata like holding and sucking. Then, accommodation refers to a process in which children create a new schema or modify an existing one in order to cope with a new object or unfamiliar situation or interact with a familiar object in a new pattern. For example, a small girl knows a dog. She happens to see a cow and thinks it is a big dog. Later, she learns to differentiate a cow from a dog. This change implies that she has developed a new schema. She acquired it by the function of accommodation. In sum, Piaget presupposed that children with no innate schema become intelligent

---

[2] The schema of conservation refers to the comprehension of children that the quantity of a certain substance such as water is conserved without change even though the form of the substance is changed due to the different forms of containers. Regardless of whether someone put one liter of water in a narrow or wide base, the quantity of the water in either base is the same. Four- to six-year-old children without the schema of conservation think that the quantity of water in the narrow vase is greater than that in the wide vase, as the level of water in the former is higher than in the latter.

as well as moral through the construction of cognitive schemata in the course of development with the innate functions, i.e., assimilation and accommodation.

What makes the ideas of Piaget, unlike Freud, on human nature look positive? Both Piaget and Freud suggested that neonates are amoral. Furthermore, Piaget and Inhelder (1969) agreed with Freud regarding the formation of conscience and superego in the mind of children, although they found the origins of these concepts in the work of Baldwin (p. 122), not Freud. Like Freud, they also acknowledged the formation of complicated emotional states in children such as a mixture of affection and hostility in their relationships with parents. However, unlike Freud, Piaget suggested that the morality of children is supposed to develop in more diverse and profound manners including the experience of mutual respect and reciprocal interactions with peers. From the Piagetian view, the unidirectional process of internalization in which children accept the moral norms and ideals of parents cannot sufficiently account for the moral development of children. The cooperation and mutuality among children as equals enable them to become genuinely moral (Piaget, 1932). With this mature morality, children are not simply following the rules established by adults, but able to modify or generate new rules for the betterment of their activities. In this sense, Piaget seemed to view human nature as more positive and constructive than Freud. According to Piaget, in sum, children do not simply receive the commandments of adults but also freely exercise their social and intellectual capacities to cooperate with others for the construction of effective rules and the realization of moral ideals.

Skinner: Three Types of Selection

According to Hoffman (1970), behaviorists or learning theorists view that the moral quality of human neonates is neither sinful nor virtuous and their mind is like a *tabula rasa,* on which nothing is already written but anything can be eventually recorded. From this description, the human mind at birth seems to be value neutral or empty. Despite this widespread impression in the behavioristic approach, Skinner did not consider the brain of an infant to be like an empty chalkboard. "The organism is, of course, not empty, and it cannot be adequately treated simply as a black box, but we must carefully distinguish between what is known about what is inside and what is merely inferred" (Skinner, 1974, p. 159). He denied clearly the idea of *tabula rasa* in terms of the contents of the human mind. More importantly, however, he did not believe that psychologists can understand fully what is inside humans by introspection, i.e., an examination of one's own perceptions, thoughts, moods, feelings, and processes. What is happening in the brain of human beings can be scarcely grasped by their observing themselves inwardly, but can be conjectured and deduced by examining the associations between concrete behaviors and consequences (Skinner, 1974).

The belief of Skinner on the limitation of the human capacity for introspection is directly applied to moral reasoning. Above all, according to him, no human judgments and behaviors can be good or bad due to their intrinsic nature (Skinner, 1971, p. 113). As humans cannot fathom deeply their own inner world, they can never make a moral judgment based on the internal values of their ideas and motivations. Instead, they simply name some behaviors moral because they result in benefits and/or remove certain negative conditions. Furthermore, there can be no fundamental difference between moral and non-moral behaviors according to this theory, as the principles of reinforcements and punishments govern both moral and non-moral behaviors. As Skinner devalues the human capacity for introspection and the particular values of morality, this approach seems to view human nature as morally neutral or unknowable.

Nonetheless, the ideas of Skinner on moral development should be examined from his broad vision of human development. He maintained that many intellectuals falsely understood his behaviorism. One of the common misunderstandings is that behaviorism ignores the influence of evolution on humans because it deals only with human behaviors in current conditions (Skinner,

1974). In fact, he incorporated the theory of evolution when he explained human development as selection by consequences (Skinner, 1981). He suggested the three types of selection with which he could explain the developmental process of human beings. The first type is natural selection; the second, operant conditioning; and, the third, the evolution of social environments or cultures. Although the idea of operant conditioning is the core component of his theory, Skinner considered seriously the theory of natural selection and integrated it into his theory of human development. This idea makes clear what Skinner thought about the condition of new born babies. Their mind is not empty, as human organisms are endowed with biological and social repertoires such as eating and sexual behavior due to natural selection (Skinner, 1981). As infants have these repertoires as innate human capacities, they never begin their lives in a perfect vacuum according to his theory. Then, it can be also asked of him whether these inborn behaviors include morals.

Unlike Freud and Piaget, who view the nature of infants as amoral, Skinner did not clearly deny the presence of certain morals as a part of the innate social repertoires which are developed through human evolution. When he explained the cause of altruism, he suggested three possibilities according to the three types of selection.

> [A]ltruistic behavior (i) may evolve through, say, kin selection; (ii) may be shaped and maintained by contingencies of reinforcement arranged by those for whom the behavior works an advantage; or (iii) may be generated by cultures, for example, induce individuals to suffer or die as heroes or martyrs (Skinner, 1981, p. 503).

In the explanation of an altruistic human behavior, there are three different levels of selection such as natural selection, individual selection (i.e., operant conditioning), and social or cultural selection. Basically, these three selections work independently and interdependently. It is, thus, possible that certain behaviors take place solely according to programs in the genes of humans. Since Skinner viewed the natural selection of humans in the process of evolution as one of the authentic ways to acquire human behaviors, human beings could commit themselves to altruistic and other moral behaviors due to the conditions developed by kin selection without the intervention of environmental forces. Then, it can be said that Skinner acknowledged the presence of innate morals in humans which are genetically transmitted. Unlike the classification of Hoffman, therefore, Skinner endorsed a presence of innate morals contrary to Freud and Piaget.

The approach of Skinner certainly differs from Piaget. Skinner, in contrast to Piaget, did not think that the human mind is equipped with the invariant functions to formulate intelligence but with an ability to behave in accordance with environmental stimuli and to modify behaviors by reinforcements (Skinner, 1981, p. 503). Piaget (1932; Piaget & Inhelder, 1969) explicitly pointed out the active and creative features of children's intelligence in the construction of moral judgments and sentiments through their interactions with parents and peers, whereas Skinner thought that human imagination or hypothetical invention cannot be considered to be causes for the development of behaviors. For him, behaviors are determined by the contingencies of reinforcement. The contingencies of reinforcement are comprised of three factors; 1) events upon which behaviors (or responses) occur, 2) the behaviors, 3) the reinforcing consequences which follow the behaviors. The interrelationships among the three factors are defined as the contingencies of reinforcement (see Skinner, 2013.) In the theory of Skinner, thus, there is not much room for intentional and creative human endeavors in the process of moral development. Unlike Piaget, Skinner did not analyze seriously and concretely the capacities of individuals to reflect on the implications of their social interactions and construct new cognitive structures to adapt themselves to the world in an original and creative manner.

As Skinner tends to doubt the importance and accuracy of our understanding of the interior world of humans, his ideas are incompatible not only with the cognitive theory of Piaget but also with the psychoanalysis of Freud. However, the mechanism of behaviorism resonates well with the pleasure principle of Freud, i.e., the instinctive pursuit of pleasure to gratify basic needs (1923, 1930, see Hoffman, 1970; Turiel, 1983). The principle of the selection of behavior depends mainly on survival values, i.e., the satisfaction of instinctual needs (see Skinner, 1981, 2013). In the end, it is important to notice that moral values do not differ from non-moral values in the mind of Skinner. People simply have identified as good or moral certain behaviors which promote their survival. In sum, Skinner acknowledged the innate morals of humans due to natural selection but disregarded the presence of the inherent values of morality and the unique mechanisms of moral development.

Contemporary Studies on Innate Morals

Quite a few contemporary psychologists still study the issue of the innate morality of human beings with creative research designs. Among developmental psychologists, Wynn and her colleagues (2018) suggested that infants are born with morals. They supported so-called moral nativism which plainly indicates that certain morals are innate in human infants. Without any socialization or learning process, young children possess moral senses from the beginning of life. These researchers maintained that they found evidence for innate morals. For instance, Bloom (2013) suggested that infants, who cannot walk and talk, are able to distinguish good behaviors from bad ones, based on the research findings of Wynn's colleagues (Hamlin et al., 2010; Hamlin et al., 2011; Wynn & Bloom, 2013). These developmental psychologists study the innate morals of human beings mainly by observing and testing the reactions and preferences of infants in diverse experimental settings. It is positive that they try to go beyond the level of abstract debate on human nature with scientific methods to verify the presence of innate morals in humans.

Hamlin and Wynn (2011) conducted experiments with five- to nine-month-old infants in order to study the preference of infants between prosocial and antisocial behaviors. They performed a puppet show in front of the infants and verified their reactions. In the show, a protagonist (an animal hand puppet) found it difficult to open the cover of a plastic box, which was very big compared to the body of the protagonist. As the box was transparent, the infants who watched the show were able to see a rattle with bright color inside the box, which was assumed to be attractive to them. In this situation, two other puppets were presented. One helped the protagonist to open the box (the "Opener"), whereas the other slammed the cover of the box to close it (the "Closer"). After the puppet show, an experimenter presented the two puppets to the infants and invited them to choose one of the two. The result was that the majority of infants selected the Opener rather than the Closer. Thus, the researchers concluded that infants tended to prefer those who help others in their goal-oriented behavior (i.e., their attempt to open the box in order to get the rattle at the experiment), and suggested that those infants made a judgment on the behaviors of the puppets as good or bad.

Based on this type of research, Wynn and her colleagues (Bloom, 2013; Hamlin & Wynn, 2011; Wynn & Bloom, 2013) argued against the philosophers and psychologists who viewed human nature as a *tabula rasa* (i.e., blank slate) and confirmed that human beings have innate moral senses. Nevertheless, they did acknowledge that their nativist approach has not yet arrived at the conclusion of innate morality in human beings. Instead, they took their opinion about the presence of innate morals in humans as an empirical proposition to be verified. Wynn and Bloom (2013) explained the implications of their findings.

> The sentiments and evaluations we have reviewed do not comprise a full-fledged system of moral reasoning. . . still, what we *do* find—the capacity to evaluate an individual's social action as positive or negative, and to generate attitudes toward others based on these evaluations—comprises an essential basis of any moral system that will eventually contain more abstract concepts of right and wrong. (p. 451)

Their evaluations on their studies seem to be reasonably modest and prudent. To incorporate this sort of contribution into the studies of moral development from a cognitive developmental perspective, it is necessary to examine the theoretical perspectives and assumptions of these contemporary psychologists who study the presence of innate morals.

Perspectives on Innate Morals: Developmental and Evolutionary

Wynn and Bloom (2013) suggested that the dispositions and capacities of infants regarding the evaluation of social interactions become a foundation for the moral development of children and adults. They developed their arguments based on the empirical findings of age differences during infancy regarding the assessment of prosocial, neutral, and antisocial behaviors (Wynn & Bloom, 2013, p. 445). There were consistencies as well as inconsistencies among infants regarding their preferences in terms of the moral qualities of characters. On the one hand, three-month-old infants as well as older infants were more likely to select a neutral character than an antisocial one. On the other hand, the three-month-old infants did not show any preferences toward a prosocial character compared to a neutral one, whereas the older tended to prefer the prosocial one. From these results, they assumed that the recognitions of antisocial behaviors appear in advance of those of prosocial ones. The negative aspects of social interactions seem to become salient to infants prior to the positive features of interactions. Such findings on age differences may not give an answer to the question of innate morals, but they do throw light on the developmental path of children, which can enrich future studies of moral development.

While Wynn and Bloom (2013) conducted studies from a developmental perspective, they also maintained that their perspective is evolutionary. They did not simply suggest that certain morals could be found in infants without any learning process, but also that some innate moral dispositions and inclinations might appear not in childhood but only in adulthood (Wynn & Bloom, 2013, p. 436). This implies that certain programs of moral development are encoded in the genes of human beings and moral development takes place according to these innate programs during the course of life. Thus, some morals may show up from the beginning of life, whereas others, at other periods of life. In fact, their approach is similar to the maturation theory of Arnold Gesell (1940), which suggests that the inherent mechanisms of human maturation regulate the basic progressions of behavior development (p. 13, see Gordon & Browne, 2013). From this view, the main factor of development is biological maturation based on inherent programs of human development. The experience of social interactions and the conditions of environments cannot influence the developmental sequence of behaviors. As Wynn and Bloom maintained that innate morals may appear at the corresponding periods of life independently of the experience of social activities, it is assumed that the inherent, maturational mechanisms of humans are mainly responsible for moral development. However, it remains ambiguous how to verify whether inherent mechanisms decide the emergence of moral behaviors and how to explain that human interactions such as discipline and cooperation or environmental factors such as school and family play no crucial roles in the moral development of humans.

The Presence of Innate Morals vs. the Early Appearance of Morals

Wynn and her colleagues speculated that some moral tendencies and proclivities are innate and inherited as they are found in the behaviors of small babies. This approach may not be valid methodologically as well as theoretically. First of all, when evolutionary psychologists study the innate morals of humans, they do not simply observe the behaviors of human infants but compare their behaviors with those of primates (see Jensen & Silk, 2013; Tomasello, 2014, 2018). They examine the social behaviors of both species such as cooperation and altruism and figure out the unique forms of human behaviors which may be explained exclusively by the evolutionary nature of human morality. (See Ch. 2 for the further explanation of the evolutionary studies on morality in this book.) What they find from those comparative studies may differ in validity from the results of the experiments with infants alone.

Secondly, like Wynn and her colleagues, Skinner integrated some aspects of evolution theories into his behaviorism and suggested that some moral behaviors are evolved by natural selection and inherited from generation to generation. Unlike them, however, he suggested there are different types of operations for human development; evolutionary, individual, and social (Skinner, 1981). In his theory, the evolutionary process, not the individual development after birth, is connected to the innate morals of humans. Thus, it might not be logically valid if some adopt findings from the developmental studies of infants as proofs for evolutionary arguments. Thus, it seems to be crucial to evaluate the studies of evolutionary biology and psychology rather than developmental studies to confront the question of innate morals. Otherwise, analyses and discussions on human nature may not go beyond the level of abstract discussions on this issue.

The Multifaceted Nature of Morality

While Wynn and her colleagues conducted their studies on morality from developmental and evolutionary perspectives, they uniquely combined various ideas from diverse sources and perspectives. This tendency can be captured well in their understanding of human nature. When Bloom (2013) argued for the presence of innate morals, he indicated that the good and right features of infants were not the sole indicator of human nature. According to him, immorality and neutrality or indifference are innate along with morality: Human beings are "by nature indifferent, even hostile to strangers" (Bloom, 2013, p. 6). His argument for the presence of innate morals within infants does not imply the purity or goodness of human nature. Instead, he claimed that human nature is multifaceted by maintaining all the three possible positions about human nature, i.e., positive, negative, and neutral (see Wynn et al., 2018).

In conjunction with the idea of a multifaceted human nature, Wynn and Bloom (2013) maintained the resemblance between infants and adults in terms of morality as follows.

In all these ways, infants' and toddlers' social judgments and responses bear a strong resemblance to those of adults. The early emergence of the evaluation of social actions—present already by 3 months of age—suggests that this capacity cannot result entirely from experience in particular cultural environments or exposure to specific linguistic practices, and it suggests that there are innate bases that ground some components of our moral cognition. (p. 450)

As children are occasionally good, bad, or indifferent, they are not very different from adults. Although they did not argue that all the physical and psychological elements of an organism are already present in its germ cells like a miniature of the organism (see Maienschein, 2017; Josi et al., 2018), Wynn and Bloom (2013) maintained that adults can be moral because they started as moral babies (p. 451). They made this unclear statement, while suggesting the idea of innate morals by using expression "moral babies." It is commonsensically agreeable that there are similarities or continuities between children and adults. This common sense, however, might not be compatible with the approach of many scholars in the area of child development, because they focus on not only continuities but also discontinuities between children and adults.

Morality from the Children's Point of View

Piaget and Inhelder (1969) stated that adults have started their life as children in the preface of the book *The Psychology of the Child*. To get to know the morality of adults, researchers need to know the morality or premorality of children. In the studies of children, it is important to interpret the behaviors of children from their own point of view, not from the perspectives of adults. Some behaviors of children may look moral or immoral, or prosocial or antisocial in the eyes of adults. Nevertheless, children may not have any intentions which adults think children possess. Damon (1988) suggested that the moral implications of actions may change along with the course of human development. From the perspectives of adults, some actions of children can be seen as morally good or bad, although children do not have any moral intentions but behave according to non-moral motives. Thus, it is crucial to find a way to enter into the inner world of children for the correct and coherent evaluation of the judgments and behaviors of children.

Damon (1980) made an argument regarding the results of the research of Hartshorne and May in the late 1920s. These researchers studied the honesty of children, which was measured by the cheating behaviors of children in various situations such as academic tests and games. They could not find a high level of consistency in the behaviors of children. For instance, a child who did not cheat at a game cheated at an academic test. Thus, they arrived at the conclusion that the morality of children was likely determined by the context of their behaviors. For children without the interior capacity of self-control, the external regulation and inhibition of authority figures seemed to be the inevitable conclusion of moral education. However, their interpretation and result were criticized by Damon and many others (see Turiel, 1983), as Hartshorne and May did not examine the inner world of children. Although the adult researchers considered cheating immoral, children in the experiments might view it as a sort of cooperation or mutual help among friends in order to do well together in the game or test (Damon, 1988). Unfortunately, the experimenters did not deal with the reasoning processes and judgments underlying the behaviors of children, they simply measured the rates of some children' behaviors.

Piaget (1932) and other researchers (Kohlberg, 1968; Turiel, 1983) from a cognitive developmental perspective tried to study how children think about and judge morally relevant issues. Kohlberg (1968) viewed children as moral philosophers and acknowledged that they have a capacity to construct moral concepts like an adult. Thus, he tried to examine the characteristics of children's interior dimension such as the logic of thinking and the underlying reasons of judgements. As this intellectual capacity exists invariantly throughout the developmental process from childhood, it can be said that he pointed out the continuity between children and adults. On the other hand, he did not intend that there are no qualitative differences of morality between children and adults. He did deal with discontinuities between infants and adults and suggested the six stages of moral development. Due to his understanding of the unique features of stages, he could explain how children become moral in a human society and how adults help children to grow up with a healthy moral consciousness. Like the example of Kohlberg's approach, therefore, researchers on moral development should pay attention to both variant and invariant aspects during the course of life and analyze the inner dimension of judgments and actions in order to establish a comprehensive theory of human growth.

2

Does Evolution Make Humans Moral?

The moral nature of man has reached its present standard, partly through the advancement of his reasoning powers and consequently of a just public opinion, but especially from his sympathies having been rendered more tender and widely diffused through the effects of habit, example, instruction, and reflection. It is not improbable that after long practice virtuous tendencies may be inherited. (Darwin, 1874, p. 382)

Charles Darwin (1809-1882), an English biologist and naturalist known for his theory of evolution, reflected on the issue of morality in his book *The descent of man.* He suggested that the human race had developed morality through the history of evolution with the aid of sympathy, reasoning, and other unique human qualities (Darwin, 1874, pp. 78−79). His view on moral development seems to be broad and balanced. First, his perspective on human morals is extensive. While Darwin (1874) certainly assumed that morality is at least partially inheritable, he did not consider natural selection as the sole factor for the formation of morality but also acknowledged the importance of interactions among humans in a tribe or community such as approval, learning, and religion for the development of morality (p. 90). Secondly, he maintained a good balance between reasoning and emotions by treating both as fundamental contributors to moral development. The rational capacity and sympathy of humans are important factors for this developmental process in humans. This integrated view of moral development seems to be a good standard according to which readers evaluate the quality of the works of evolutionary scientists on morals.

A good number of researchers in various fields such as biology and psychology have studied the influence of evolution on human morality. This issue is extremely difficult to study because the development of morality in the evolution history of humans is hard to trace by any physical evidence. Despite this challenge, some scientists observed the altruistic behaviors of humans and animals and suggested certain common features as the basis of their theoretical conceptualizations on human morality (see Wilson, 1975), and others conducted comparative studies on the cooperation of human beings and animals to identify unique factors for the sociality and morality of humans (see Vaish & Tomasello, 2013). For me, it is intriguing to see whether they take an integrated perspective on this issue as Darwin did. Do they consider the influence of evolution in both its biological and sociological dimensions? Do they study the roles of both emotion and rationality in the evolution of human morality? In this chapter, I would like to verify whether important ideas regarding the influence of evolution on morality are based on evidence from an empirical study with a logical perspective and a reliable method.

First, I will deal with the ideas of epigenesis and preformation as the two contrasting approaches to the development of an organism. As a perspective on the nature of human development influences the evaluation of scientific findings, I would like to discuss which approach between the two is realistic and conducive to the studies of moral development. Secondly, I will review the sociobiology of Wilson (1975). My interests are centered on the question of whether his understanding of morality is leaning toward a genetic determinism. Thirdly, I will examine the challenges and limitations of the evolutionary studies on the evolutionary roots of human morality. Fourthly, I will explain the comparative studies between humans and great apes by Tomasello and his colleagues (see Tomasello, 2014; Tomasello et al., 2012; Vaish & Tomasello, 2013; Warneken et al., 2006). Lastly, I will discuss the role of cooperation in the moral development of humans. This issue can relate the ideas of Piaget on children's morality to the experimental findings of the comparative studies. By dealing with these themes, I would like to help the consumers of the publications of evolutionary science on the social nature of humans to evaluate and discern them in a critical and constructive manner.

Epigenesis and Preformation

Theoretical approaches to the nature of human development can be categorized into two contrasting ideas; epigenesis and preformation. These ideas come from embryology, which is classified as a discipline of biology that deals with the formation and development of the embryo and fetus. The theory of epigenesis claims that an organism such as a plant and an animal develops from a seed or egg through a sequence of stages in which the cells differentiate and the organs are formed, whereas preformationism (or preformism) maintains that all the physical and psychic elements of an organism are already present in the germ cells as a miniature of the organism (Maienschein, 2017; Wessel, 2009; see Josi et al., 2018). The majority of researchers in the field of developmental science follow the idea of epigenesis since they examine systematic variations in the cognitive, emotional, and moral development of children and adolescents. The premises of these researchers could be summarized as follows: Human development takes place by formulating and modifying cognitive structures, emotional expressions, and social behaviors throughout the path of life from the individual's birth.

Epigenesis and Morality

Above all, Piaget (1971), as a pioneering scholar in the studies of morality from a cognitive developmental perspective, considered the epigenetic process to be the basis of intellectual operations (p. 23). In this context, "epi" means "after," and "genetic" implies what concerns generation, that is, the principle for the life of a human being. Thus, the epigenetic process means the developmental process of an individual human being after the beginning of its life. In the epigenetic process, children construct and transform knowledge through their interactions with the environment. As morality is understood as an essential part of human knowledge (Piaget, 1932; Kohlberg, 1969) or a domain of social reasoning (Smetana, 2006; Turiel, 1983, 2006), the epigenetic approach has been the main thread of moral development studies. In short, the cognitive developmental approach presupposes that the human capacity of moral reasoning is not formed before birth but develops in the mind of children and adolescents through the course of life.

The idea of epigenesis enables researchers to find a right focus in the studies of moral development without falling into a determinism. According to the epigenesis theory, any structures of moral cognition and emotion do not exist in the genes of human beings. There are neither moral genes nor the master plan of moral development inscribed in the DNA. Even though epigenesis negates neither the significance of heredity nor the influence of evolution, it rejects any type of genetic determinism, which argues that human development is predominantly and precisely regulated by the genes of an individual. Instead, epigenesis denotes that the formation of cognitive schemata including morality occurs in the interaction between organism and environment through the stages of development after birth (see Piaget, 1971). On the other hand, the concept of epigenesis is not compatible with the environmental determinism which disregards the mutual influence and reciprocal interaction between organism and environment for development. The social and physical environments such as parents, peers, social media, school, etc. do not dictate all the features of the moral development of children. Although they are present in and influenced by a specific environmental setting, children are not the passive recipients of preformed knowledge and existing norms in their community and society, but the active constructors of morality who engage themselves in interactions with their social and physical surroundings. Therefore, the study of moral development within an epigenetic approach should be free from both genetic and environmental determinisms but pursue the comprehension of the emergence and transformation of children's morals in the context of child-environment interaction.

Classical and Modern Preformism

According to Wessel (2009), "Modern preformism considers DNA to be the functional equivalent to a plan which provides the specific information to govern the structures and development of an individual organism" (p. 35). He differentiated modern preformism from a classical one. In general, a traditional preformation theory claims that the structures of an organism are already formed in its germ cells and appear during the course of its life. Instead, a modern preformism acquires a more sophisticated form, which suggests not the presence of the structures of an organism, but the developmental program of the organism in its genes. In other words, this view of preformation suggests that the phenotype of an organism, which refers to observable characteristics of an individual, depends solely on its genotype, which corresponds to the genetic heritage written in the DNA. When this idea is applied to the cognitive development of human beings, the preformation of cognition implies that the development of intellectual structures takes place only by the realization of genotypic programs. According to the modern preformism, the master plan of the development of intellectual structures is already formed in the genes of a fetus.

In the same vein, the preformation theory of morality presupposes that the morality of a human being is innately present in a complete manner prior to a process of learning and growth. This idea differs from the theory of Skinner (1981). He did mention the possibility of some innate morals due to the natural selection of human species through evolution. However, he did not consider natural selection to be the sole mechanism of human development, but included the mechanism of individual selection (i.e., operant conditioning) as well as the role of social and cultural forces in human development. Unlike this theory, the radical ideas of preformation envision the presence of innate morals in a complete manner. One of the main problems of preformism lies in the lack of reliable evidence. Although some have initiated scientific endeavors based on preformism, any sorts of empirical studies regarding human genes have not yet verified any innate structures or designs for complex mental activities like moral reasoning. Thus, the ideas of preformation appear to be ambiguous and questionable (see Wessel, 2009). As long as contemporary studies in embryology remain in this state, it may be neither helpful nor productive to adopt the ideas of preformation for the discussions on the evolutionary influence on moral development.

Morality and Genetic Determination

One of the founding figures in the line of evolutionary studies in morality is Edward O. Wilson. As an entomologist, he has studied the social dimensions of insects such as ants and founded a new discipline, which is named sociobiology, as a branch of evolutionary biology. Wilson (1978) defined sociobiology as "the systematic study of the biological basis of all forms of social behavior, in all kinds of organisms, including man" (p. 16). One of the social behaviors in his study is morality. He explained his ideas of morality mainly by focusing on the altruistic behaviors of animals as well as humans. The principal idea of his theory is that human morality is determined by natural selection. As a result of natural selection, the limbic system of the brain regulates the emotional reactions of humans (e.g., fear) which, in turn, constrain moral behaviors. It implies that emotion, not rationality, is primarily responsible for human morality. Wilson has influenced directly and indirectly some psychologists to appreciate the relevance of evolutionary studies for a comprehensive understanding of human morality by maintain the primary role of emotions in morality (see Haidt, 2001; cf. Tomasello, 2014).

According to Wilson (1978), natural selection aims at the transmission of genes rather than the survival of an organism. In the process of natural selection, human morality such as altruism is programmed in the genes so that the genes can be transmitted to the next generation of humans. In his theory, altruism is defined as "behavior that benefits others at the cost of the lifetime production of offspring by the altruist" (Wilson & Hölldobler, 2005, p. 13367). The altruistic behavior of an organism increases the number of offspring that others are likely to produce, but reduces the number of its own. This altruistic disposition is inscribed in the genes of human beings and used like a tool for the preservation of the genes in subsequent generations. As he believed that human moral behaviors are directly controlled by the genes of individuals, his theory of morality seems to be a genetic determinism.

Then, what is the nature of morality according to sociobiology? Morality is an instinct (Wilson, 1978, p. 5). Human beings become moral principally not because of education or discipline, but because of the instinct which is an inherited capacity. Human ethical premises and practices are predominantly and profoundly determined by innate programs in the genes. The players of these programs of morality are the emotions and motivations which tend to be automatic reactions to stimuli from the environment. Human morality as an innate self-regulating capacity is transmitted across generations. Wilson's theory of morality seems to be leaning toward the idea of preformation: Morality is fully formed in the genes of an organism. From this view, what humans experience during the course of life does not seem to be crucial for the development of morality, since what is programmed in the genes makes the organism moral.

Dual Track of Human Social Evolution

Wilson (1978) tried to acknowledge the influence of social environment by suggesting the idea of the dual track of human social evolution. It refers to the biological and cultural evolution which makes humans live together with ethical norms. The social behaviors of humans are shaped by the influence of their genes and their interactions with a cultural environment. Thus, Wilson apparently extended the evolutionary theory of biology into the sphere of culture and explained the interactions between the two types of evolution. However, these two types are not equal in their relationship in the mind of Wilson. He described the relation between the two with a "leash" metaphor: "The genes hold culture on a leash. The leash is very long, but inevitably values will be constrained in accordance with their effects on the human gene pool" (Wilson, 1978, p. 167). Genes take a primary position in evolution and regulate the influence of culture on evolution. The products of cultures and the direction of cultural evolution are basically controlled by the behavioral dispositions of humans which are deeply rooted in the genes.

Furthermore, the thoughts of Wilson about morality, religion, and mythology are likely to make his perspective on the nature of cultural influence rather ambiguous and uncertain. The human mind could create ideas about morals, religion, and myth according to the inherited memories in the brain without any input from the environment (Wilson, 1978, p. 200). As the capacity of a human brain reaches the level of self-sufficiency to recall and contrive the image and ideas of morality from its storage of memories, cultural changes do not seem to play an essential role in moral development. Due to the lack of clarity in the elaboration of the impact of social interactions on moral development in his theory, his ideas on the influence of natural selection on morality can hardly be integrated in a harmonious way with any theories on moral development, which acknowledge the role of social interactions (cf. Kohlberg, 1981; Piaget, 1930; Turiel, 1983).

Natural Selection and Altruism

The main theme of Wilson's theory centers on the question of how altruism evolves by natural selection. According to him, "Natural selection is the process whereby certain genes gain representation in the following generations superior to that of other genes located at the same chromosome positions" (Wilson, 1975, p. 3). Organisms with certain genes tend to survive more become more common in the following generations than those with other genes. The altruistic behaviors of an organism, however, seem to be far from this principle as they reduce its own benefits or often cost even its life. Despite this apparent contradiction, Wilson (1975) confirmed that the natural selection of altruistic behaviors is found in social animals including the human species and he presented some examples from the lives of insects. For instance, soldiers among ants and termites defend their nests despite a serious danger. In this situation, those ants risk or lose their own lives for the safety or survival of others. As the altruistic behaviors of individual ants contribute to the preservation and transmission of the genes of their species, natural selection has been operating to facilitate the evolution of a genetic predisposition to altruism.

Wilson and his colleagues created a major long-lasting controversy regarding the main type of natural selection for social and altruistic behaviors. They maintained that the principal mechanism or force which enables altruistic behaviors is group selection rather than kin selection. (See Nowak et al., 2010; Wilson, 1975, 1978, 2005, 2012; Wilson & Hölldobler, 2005.) Group selection implies that individual organisms act altruistically for the survival of their group when it competes with another group, whereas kin selection implies that an organism acts for the multiplication of its relatives at the cost of its own fitness or survival. His idea of group selection has been accepted by some evolutionary biologists and psychologists and developed into multilevel selection theory, i.e., natural selection occurs in the multiple levels of biological organization such as cells, individuals, and groups (see Graham et al., la 2013; D. S. Wilson & Dugatkin, 1997; D. S. Wilson & Sober, 1994; D. S. Wilson & Wilson, 2007). On the other hand, a good number of evolutionary scientists criticized the idea of group selection or multilevel selection theory. For instance, West et al. (2007) argued that the use of the term "group selection" leads to a semantic confusion and is less helpful for empirical research, and they recommended the use of the term "kin selection," as its formula includes the concept of group selection (see also Abbot et al., 2011; Henriques, 2008, 2011, 2013; Pinker, 2015). The controversy between kin selection and group selection may not be easily resolved, although there are attempts to integrate the two positions (see Kramer & Meunier, 2016).

Lastly, it is necessary to verify the authenticity of the theory of Wilson by examining the evidence which he has provided to support his theory. His research methods consisted mainly of naturalistic observations. He observed the behaviors of ants and bees and constructed his sociobiology. Evolutionary psychologists Jensen and Silk (2013) made a comment on the limitation of the observational method. They suggested, "Behavioral observations provide good evidence that altruism is relatively common in nature, but observations alone provide little insight about the mechanisms that underlie these behaviors" (Jensen & Silk, 2013, p. 416). According to this comment, it is impossible to verify whether the underlying mechanisms of animal social behaviors are comparable and equivalent to those of human social behaviors by simply identifying the common external features of behaviors between the two. Thus, it would be difficult to reach any scientific conclusions regarding the nature of human and animal altruistic behaviors from Wilson's approach.

Evolutionary Studies of Morality

Evolutionary psychologists and biologists initiate their studies on the evolutionary roots of human morality by acknowledging challenges and limitations of empirical studies. Above all, they could not find the traces of moral reasoning by the analyses of the genes of human beings (Jensen & Silk, 2013). This limitation of direct investigation of the presence of morality in the body of human beings made them resort to comparative studies of morality between human beings and animals. Among various animals, many evolutionary psychologists focus on the question of whether human infants share any morally relevant features with other primates such as chimpanzees and baboons. It is known that humans and chimpanzees have a common ancestor about seven million years ago. The genetic difference between the two is about 1.2 percent (*How Do We Know Humans Are Primates?*, 2010). This seemingly small difference has been the focus of evolutionary scientists. They examine particular characteristics of modern humans such as bipedalism with a premise that these unique human traits evolved after the separation between humans and other primates. In the same vein, the evolutionary psychologists try to comprehend what makes human morality unique and how the foundations of morality evolved. They pursue these goals by comparing the common and different features of social behaviors between humans and great apes (see Jensen & Silk, 2013, Tomasello, 2014). This academic endeavor is stimulating as well as challenging.

It is certainly complicated to interpret the behaviors of infants and toddlers, those of animals, and the difference between the two. Evolutionary studies, nevertheless, seem to be one of the most reliable approaches in dealing with the question of the innate morals of humans and the influence of evolution on human morality.

Difficulties in the Interpretation of Animal Behaviors

Jensen and Silk (2013) concluded that studies have not discovered sufficient evidence to prove the presence of the moral reasoning capacity or morally relevant emotions in animals. Although there has been a good deal of observation on helping and altruistic behaviors among great apes, these behaviors are not replicated in a consistent manner in experimental studies. For instance, Seyfarth and Cheney (1984) found that vervet monkeys are willing to help the members of another group which have groomed them in the recent past more than the genetically closely related monkeys which have done the same to them. A helping behavior as a response to a grooming episode may not be frequently observed among the kin of the monkeys because these sorts of affinitive behaviors like grooming tend to take place commonly and regularly among them. They become habituated to these behaviors and less responsive to them. Instead, the grooming bout of a non-kin monkey can be rather significant and stimulating to the beneficiary because it occurs rarely. It is, however, difficult to confirm the interpretation of the grooming episodes by Seyfarth and Cheney (1984) because it is not firmly based on the comprehension of the exact nature of the underlying psychological mechanisms of these behaviors. Moreover, these behavioral patterns are not found in experimental settings (Jensen & Silk, 2013). What can be confirmed from these results is somewhat limited and too general. It can be said that social relationships or interactions in the past influence the helping behaviors of monkeys. Thus, this difficulty also becomes a challenge to comparative studies between humans and non-human primates in regard to altruistic behaviors. Because it is complicated to understand the nature of the altruistic behaviors of nonhuman primates, the comparison of human behaviors to theirs easily becomes superficial or unfounded.

In addition, Jensen and Silk (2013) noticed certain limitations and confusions in the studies of empathy among nonhuman primates and other animals. There are quite a few observations of helping behaviors of animals for another animal in distress. For instance, De Waal (2009) explained the empathy of primates with an example from his observations. In a zoo, a bonobo saw a frightened bird due to an accident, approached the bird, and let it fly away. He suggested that the bonobo probably knew about the nature of birds from its experience, that is, the birds are flying with feathers. Based on this knowledge and the real encounter with the bird which could not fly, the bonobo understood the distress of the bird and its desire to fly at that moment, and reacted to help the bird fly away. Thus, this behavior was suggested to be an example of empathy in both cognitive and emotional senses. However, Jensen and Silk (2013) suggested that the interpretation of this behavior can vary. Especially, it is not clear whether that sort of behavior was motivated by empathy or curiosity. In the example of de Waal, the bonobo could do all those actions due to curiosity without perceiving any pain of the bird.

To verify the underlying motives of the helping behaviors of animals, Jensen and Silk (2013) made a distinction between empathy and emotional contagion or personal distress (see Eisenberg, 2002; Eisenberg et al., 2010; Hoffman, 2001). Both empathy and emotional contagion are one's reactions which are similar to another person's experience and expression. Between the two, only the former includes a genuine concern for another's welfare. The latter does not have morally relevant motives, but aims to reduce its own stress. Koski and Sterck (2010) suggested that the phenomenon of emotional contagion is found among chimpanzees, but did not guarantee that fully developed empathic reactions exist among them. Therefore, the helping behavior of an animal could be understood as a reaction to reduce its own distress. In spite of the prosocial appearance, the behavior is still egoistic, not altruistic. On the other hand, researchers have not yet found any convincing evidence for the presence of empathy as a source of the altruistic behaviors of animals. Thus, it is premature to make a conclusion that animals have empathic capacities. Moreover, it is difficult to accept the ideas of some sociobioligists if they try to suggest certain behaviors of animals and insects as evidence to confirm the presence of innate altruism in humans.

Comparative Experiments between Humans and Apes

A good number of evolutionary psychologists continue to compare the behaviors of humans to those of some animals in the hope of finding the evolutionary roots of human social behaviors including morality. Particularly, Tomasello and his colleagues conducted well-designed comparative experimental studies between humans and great apes (see Tomasello, 2014; Tomasello et al., 2012; Vaish & Tomasello, 2013; Warneken et al., 2006). For instance, Warneken et al. (2006) did experiments to examine differences in cooperative activities between human children of 18-24 months and young chimpanzees. Both a child and a chimpanzee undertook four cooperative activities (games and problem-solving tasks) with a human adult partner. They were simple activities such as retrieving a toy by simultaneously opening both sides of the tube which enclosed the toy. One of the most intriguing results was found when the adult partner suddenly stopped participating in the cooperative activity. In that situation, the reactions from the two groups were different. Human children were likely to communicate with the adult partner in order to get him to engage in the activity again, whereas chimpanzees did not send any signals in an attempt to make the partner stay in the activity. Warneken et al. (2006) interpreted this difference as evidence for human cooperation with shared intentionality.

The shared intentionality of children basically describes the uniqueness of cooperation in humans. It implies that children understand the nature of collective activity. Children notice that they and other participants share the same goal, know that they have their own roles, which are independent of others' roles, and coordinate different roles to achieve the joint goal of group activity (Warneken et al., 2006). For the chimpanzees, there are no clear signs of collaboration with a shared vision and goal. They work apparently in a group. However, it is not a cooperative action with shared intentionality. According to Warneken et al. (2006), when the chimpanzees were individually rewarded in the experiment, they were able to perform the social activities with the partner. However, once they achieved what they individually wanted, such as food, they did not engage further in any cooperation. It implies that chimpanzees understood the goal of the task, but considered it as individual, not joint or shared. Instead, when the collaborative activities were finished or interrupted, children tended to restart them or invite their partner to engage in them again. The disposition of the children for collaborations was found to be authentic. They did not react passively in the context of cooperation but tried to regulate the behaviors of the adult partner for the continuation of cooperative activities. Thus, it was suggested that children value the cooperation itself, regardless of external rewards. As cooperation is known to be a foundation for moral development (Piaget, 1932), the findings and ideas of Tomasello and his colleagues on the unique features of human cooperation can be a guide to a depth analysis of the unique nature of human morals.

Cognitive Development of Human Primates

Unlike the arguments of sociobiologists on the evolutionary bases of morality which tend mainly to emphasize the role of emotions in moral judgments (see Greene & Haidt, 2002, 2003; Wilson, 1975, 2012), Tomasello and his colleagues try to explain the early development of human cognition which is essential for cooperation. Liszkowski et al. (2008) have found that even 12-month-old infants try to help an adult to find an object by pointing to the location of the object. This confirms that young children understand the goal of the actions of adults and cooperate to achieve the goal. Without engaging physically in the activity, human children can cooperate with others due to their cognitive capacities for collaboration and intentions to help others. It is inconceivable that human beings can do any social and moral behaviors without this kind of cognitive capacity. Tomasello and his colleagues confirm that human capacities for cognition and reasoning are essential and principal factors of moral development (cf. Turiel, 2006a).

Fletcher et al. (2012) studied differences in social cognition in the collaborations of three- and five-year-old children and chimpanzees. Both the children and the chimpanzees were able to work in pairs. In their studies, two individuals had to work together to solve a problem by playing different roles. The researchers used an apparatus for a marble-run game whose structure asks the cooperation of the two. One makes a ball roll down a ramp and the other pushes back a door on the ramp of the apparatus to let the ball drop (i.e., Study 1) or puts a finger into a hole to divert the ball (i.e., Study 2). In both studies, two individuals in pairs were asked to change their roles after the first set of trials. The difference between children and chimpanzees occurred in a clear manner when the roles of the two individuals were switched in Study 2. The children were likely to play the switched roles faster than their partners at the initial trials. It means that children already started to understand the roles of partners in the first trials and were able to perform them more swiftly in the second trials when the roles were switched than when they had done them initially without any exposures to the trials. While they were doing their own work, they seemed to observe the partner's activities and the mechanism of their collaboration. However, this level of cooperation was not found in the activities among non-human participants. Unlike children, they did not seem to carefully observe and comprehend the role of the partner during the initial experience of cooperation.

What is implied in the finding that chimpanzees, unlike children, were not able to perform well the switched roles in the studies of Fletcher et al. (2012)? The chimpanzees lacked the ability to have an integrated perspective on cooperative activities. By contrast, children have a unique cognitive capacity to place two different roles of the activity in one mental dimension so that they may watch and see what others do while performing their own roles. To articulate the exceptionality of human social cognition, the researchers suggested that young human children have a bird's eye view with which they construct a mental representation of the two roles of the game in an integrated manner (Fletcher et al., 2012). As if the human children observe their cooperative activities from an elevated position, they are able to integrate two different roles into a single dimension. Tomasello and his colleagues view this kind of unique human cognitive capacity, which originates from the evolution of human cooperation, as playing an important role in moral development (see Tomasello, 2014; Vaish & Tomasello, 2013).

Along with some significant findings from the comparative studies of Tomasello and his colleagues, there were also other results with uncertain implications. For example, from the works of Fletcher et al. (2012), there was no difference between three-year-old children and chimpanzees in Study 1. These two groups, unlike the group of five-year-old children, did not show the enhancement of their performances in the second trials in which their roles were switched. Only five-year-old children demonstrated the effect of learning from the first trials. In Study 2, both three- and five-year-old children did better than chimpanzees. These results were somewhat different from the expectations of the researchers. They thought that Study 2 would be more difficult than Study 1 for the participants. It turned out, however, that three-year-old children did better in Study 2 than Study 1. It is, thus, not easy to explain why the difference between three-year-old children and chimpanzees was found only in one of the two studies. This kind of complication confirms the challenging nature of comparative studies between human and animals, the importance of the consistency of the findings from the studies, and the necessity of further studies with creative research designs and methods.

The Ultrasociality of Human Beings

Tomasello makes a distinction between humans and other species not simply in the external features of collective activities but also in the underlying mechanisms of cooperation. While he accepts that social behaviors of animals and insects are genetically determined by natural selection (see also Wilson, 1975), he maintains that the particular social behaviors of humans are evolved along with "ultrasociality," that is, a type of intentionality is rooted in "some psychological mechanisms—both cognitive and motivational—that have evolved to support humans' ultra-cooperative lifeway" (Tomasello, 2014, p. 187). To explain how humans become ultra-social animals, Tomasello et al. (2012) presented the interdependence hypothesis with which they suggested two main evolutionary steps (see Tomasello, 2014; Vaish & Tomasello, 2013). According to the hypothesis, humans were forced to become collaborative foragers in the first stage, and developed new skills for collaboration facing competition with other groups in the second stage.

In the first stage of evolution, humans found themselves in a condition in which they had to be collaborative for their survival, perhaps due to ecological changes (Tomasello et al., 2012). They might have died if they had not created an interdependent way of foraging and putting it into practice. Thus, they became interdependent with one another and began to reveal a direct interest in protecting the security and wellness of their collaborators. As a result of this transformation, humans came to possess joint intentionality and know how to cooperate with helpers and avoid cheaters. The joint intentionality of humans, as a low level of shared intentionality, implies that humans were able to possess transitory motivations and skills for collaboration. The examples of this intentionality are "sharing of works and results" and "proceeding with joint goals and attention" (Tomasello et al., 2012, p. 681). It is found in a small-scale collaboration and not a fully developed type of intentionality for social life.

In the second stage, according to the interdependence hypothesis of Tomasello et al. (2012), human collaborative capacities in motivational and technical dimensions were accumulated and expanded within groups due to the competition and conflicts among the groups of humans. In this stage, humans created conventions, institutions, and cultural norms, which embodied their collective intentionality and increased a sense of belonging to their specific cultural group. In terms of shared intentionality, the second stage is characterized by the collective intentionality of humans, which is qualitatively more advanced than the joint intentionality of the first stage. Humans in the second stage perform a large-scale cooperation according to the norms and regulations of their cultural group. They begin to understand the homogenous nature of their group which is represented by social norms, cultural practices, and civil institutions (Tomasello et al., 2012, p. 684). This level of group-minded identification in humans makes their social cognition and behaviors become more interdependent, systematic, collaborative, and altruistic than the previous stage of evolution.

Tomasello and his colleagues conducted their comparative experimental studies of social behaviors of humans and other primates as well as their studies of human children (Tomasello, 2014; Tomasello et al., 2012; Vaish & Tomasello, 2013) and they formulated the interdependence hypothesis. It is important to note that they did not make the hypothesis based on the common aspects between human and non-human primates, but on the unique features of humans. In this regard, they differ from the sociobiological approach of Wilson (1975, 1978), which explained the altruism of humans by the common social behaviors of animals and humans. Instead of making a global assumption about altruism in the name of social animals, it seems to be significant to verify the uniqueness of cooperative and prosocial dispositions in humans by differentiating them from other animals and to study the developmental process of this unique human character in the course of evolution as well as in the cycle of life.

Two Dimensions of Moral Development

How could Tomasello and his colleagues prove whether this kind of evolutionary process takes place in the development of children as well as in the course of human evolution? One of the fundamental difficulties was that they could not verify this kind of hypothesis with certain archeological evidence such as fossils, or biological conditions such as genetical markers. Faced with this limitation, they turned their attention to the cognition and action of young children with the assumption that developmental changes in childhood reflect the evolutionary changes of humankind. For instance, Rakoczy et al. (2008) conducted studies with two- and three-year-old children to examine whether and how they react to the mistake of a player of simple games in different settings. They found that the children in both groups tended to react to a mistake. This result implies that young children understand the form and content of a normative behavior and the discrepancy between the normative and actual behaviors. They also found the difference between the two groups. The three-year-old children were more likely to correct the mistake in more explicit manners (e.g., indicating or correcting verbally the mistake) than the two-year-old toddlers. It implies that the older children have a greater ability than the younger to share their intentions with others and play and work collectively with them. The progress of shared intentionality and cooperation has also been treated as a main indicator of human evolution in the interdependence hypothesis of Tomasello et al. (2012).

Vaish and Tomasello (2013) introduced two dimensions of moral development to systematically explain the developmental changes of young children. They are toddlers' dyadic morality (i.e., 1 to 3 years of age) and preschoolers' norm-based morality (i.e., 3 to 5 years of age). In the first dimension, toddlers tend to show prosocial behaviors in a natural manner. It means that these young children do not internalize the implications of social norms but still demonstrate prosocial behaviors in their interpersonal relationships. These behaviors tend to be limited to the relationships with specific individuals. Vaish and Tomasello (2013) named this tendency dyadic morality or second-personal morality, because toddlers act morally mainly in the context of specific relationships, not in the wide context of social groups and communities with a comprehension of the social standards established by the community. In the second dimension, the social behaviors of children reflect the moral norms of the group, which they believe that all the group members should know and follow. These children are able to apply moral norms and judgments to others as well as themselves in an impersonal or agent-neutral manner. Their prosocial behaviors, such as helping, and moral judgments, such as punishments of wrongdoings, take place in various social relationships. Thus, children with norm-based morality, unlike the younger children, could help both their friends and strangers and judge both their own actions and others' conducts according to the same rules and principles of the community.

According to Vaish and Tomasello (2013), the two dimensions of moral development correspond to the two evolutionary steps of the interdependence hypothesis. Basically, they have assumed a correspondence between ontogeny (i.e., the developmental course of an individual organism from conception to the emergence of secondary sexual characteristics) and phylogeny (i.e., the evolutionary course of a species of organism). Specifically, the dyadic morality of toddlers as the first dimension of moral development is connected to the first stage of interdependence (i.e., a collaboration for foraging or survival), whereas the norm-based morality of preschoolers is connected to the second stage of interdependence (i.e., a large-scale cooperation based on the social norms of a cultural group). The children in the second dimension as well as humankind of the second stage begin to understand social norms, have a sense of belonging to a particular social and cultural group, and behave morally, prosocially, and cooperatively according to the norms. In the schema of Tomasello and his colleagues, thus, the course of moral development in childhood, which can be empirically verified (see Rakoczy et al., 2008; Vaish & Tomasello, 2013), replicates and supports that of moral development in the evolution of humans.

Ontogeny and Phylogeny in Moral Development

Reviewing the studies of evolutionary psychologists, it is inevitable to ask the validity of the application of the findings of studies on the moral development of children (i.e., ontogeny) to the hypothesis about the evolution of the social mentality and behaviors of humankind (i.e., phylogeny). The connection between ontogeny and phylogeny is suggested in the biogenetic rule (i.e., recapitulation theory) of Ernst Haeckel in 1866 (Medicus, 1992). According to this rule, ontogeny recapitulates phylogeny. The earlier developmental characteristics of an organism resemble the older phylogenetic features of its species, and the later developmental characteristics, the more recent phylogenetic features. This rule seems to be applied in the schema of Tomasello and his colleagues. The dyadic morality and joint intentionality as the first dimension of ontogeny represent the first stage of interdependence in phylogeny, and the norm-based morality and collective intentionality as the second dimension of ontogeny represent the second stage of interdependence in phylogeny (see Tomasello, 2014; Tomasello et al., 2012; Vaish & Tomasello, 2013). Regarding this schema, it should be asked whether this sort of connection between ontogeny and phylogeny is appropriate for understanding human social reasoning and behaviors.

Above all, the recapitulation theory is widely known to be valid for anatomy, not for social behavior or reasoning. Medicus (1992) said that the recapitulation theory is not applicable to behavioral development in general, as no empirical studies have proved the validity of this theory for it. Thus, it is dubious if anyone can apply this theory to the studies of social and moral development. This uncertainty regarding recapitulation theory is present in the schema of Tomasello and his colleagues. They associated the interdependence hypothesis regarding the evolution of human cooperation (i.e., phylogeny) with the theory of the two dimensions of moral development (i.e., ontogeny). Although the part of ontogeny in their studies can be supported by empirical proofs, their attempt to bridge ontogeny and phylogeny does not look convincing due to a lack of evidence on the part of phylogeny. While I acknowledge possible resemblances between the phylogeny and ontogeny of human sociality as an intriguing research topic, I maintain that the theoretical structure of Tomasello and his colleagues needs to be consolidated by new findings in the field of evolutionary studies.

Cooperation and Moral Development

Piagetian researchers certainly believe that the evolution of humankind has enormous effects on the generation of basic human functions such as assimilation and accommodation for cognitive and moral development. With these innate functions, children can construct social and moral schemata through their interactions with adults and peers. Piaget (1932) suggested that cooperation among peers is one of the main contributors to the development of autonomous, mature morality. Although Tomasello does not seem to follow closely the ideas of Piaget, it is noticeable that he also focuses on the significance of collaboration in his studies on morality. As a matter of fact, their approaches are different from one another regarding this topic. For instance, Tomasello dealt with cooperation among children, among animals, between children and adults, and between chimpanzees and human adults, whereas Piaget mainly thought about cooperation among children. Despite certain differences, both of them accepted the crucial role of cooperation for moral development and tried to examine the underlying cognitive and emotional processes of collaborations. Their interests in and ideas on cooperation can formulate some sophisticated questions for studies of moral development.

Above all, it is noteworthy that Tomasello and his colleagues have studied principally cooperation and shared intentionality unlike other evolutionary scientists who focus mainly on altruism. They certainly expand the horizon of evolutionary studies on morality. As they approach morality from human sociality, which is observed well in cooperation, they examine morality in the realm of human social cognition and behavior. Turiel (1983, 2002), as a Piagetian scholar, views moral thinking as a part of social reasoning and considers the coordination between moral and non-moral judgments to be crucial for the complex decision-making process of humans. Without devaluing the significance of studies on specific morally relevant behaviors and emotions such as altruism and compassion, I would like to emphasize the necessity of evolutionary research on basic social behaviors such as cooperation, distribution, communication, social reasoning, etc. Morality can be correctly understood only when it is approached with the broad and balanced vision which deals with the general context of social life as well as the particular areas of interpersonal relationships. Among the evolutionary psychologists, Tomasello and his colleagues work on moral development with an extended view on human sociality.

In terms of the relationship between morality and cooperation, the independence and interdependence between them should be carefully elaborated in studies of moral development. Although it is assumed that the experience of cooperation positively influences the growth of morals (Piaget, 1930), the association between cooperation and morality needs to be critically reviewed. On the one hand, human cooperation itself need not be viewed as moral. Clearly, quite a few individuals can cooperate for their egoistic and even immoral goals. Terrorists, gangsters, and corrupted politicians could be very collaborative among themselves. This kind of cooperation can never be considered ethically valuable. Thus, it is necessary to maintain a certain distinction between collaboration and morality. On the other hand, the reciprocal influences between the two should be tested in empirical studies. In many cases, cooperation is treated as a foundation for moral development (Piaget, 1932). However, the rudimentary or immature morality of toddlers can be a foundation for the progress of their capacities for collaboration. By introducing these points, I would like to emphasize that the relationship between cooperation and morality is one of the most valuable themes for the advance of human knowledge in terms of both ontogeny and phylogeny, and needs further elaborations and experiments with innovative research designs and methods.

3

Is Emotion More Important than Reasoning in Moral Judgments?

Kant did not consider respect to be an interpersonal feeling like affection or fear. Rather, he considered it to be a feeling resulting from a direct action of moral law on affectivity. (. . .) 'In respecting a person,' Kant said, 'I respect him insofar as he applies or embodies moral law, not as an individual as such.' Bovet squarely reverses this position. On the one hand, respect is an interpersonal feeling like any other. It is, however, a feeling composed of an element of affection (. . .) and an element of fear (. . .). Both elements are necessary; neither is sufficient by itself. On the other hand, respect conceived in this way is genetically the source, not the result, of moral law. This is because the small child agrees to obey insofar as he respects his parents. He does not begin with a consciousness of moral law detached from them and then come to respect them because they embody and impose that moral law. (Piaget, 1965, p. 301)

Most philosophers and psychologists would agree that emotions are important in moral development. Kant (1785) proposed that some feelings like respect are morally relevant because moral judgments and actions should grow out of respect for moral law. Thus, it might be a misunderstanding to think that the Kantian approach generally ignores the role of emotions in morality. In the area of psychology, Piaget (1932, 1954, 1966) also viewed a feeling of respect as a central moral affect, although he differed from Kant in that he, like Bovet, emphasized that children show respect mainly for other individuals such as parents and friends, not for the moral law. Kohlberg (1969) also emphasized the importance of moral emotions such as guilt and empathy and differentiated them from non-moral

48

emotions such as fear and anxiety. Piaget and Kohlberg, who studied moral development from a cognitive perspective, did not fail to acknowledge the importance of emotions in moral development.

Many psychologists have suggested that both cognition and emotion are involved in children's moral development (see Turiel, 2006b, 2015; Cowell & Decety, 2015; Decety et al., 2012; Decety & Howard, 2013; Malti & Ongley, 2013). Turiel (2006b) proposed that feeling and thinking reciprocally inform each other's maintenance and development. Arsenio and Lover (1995) suggested that the formation of moral principles in children takes place when they have emotional experiences and abstract the communal aspects of these experiences. Nevertheless, there seems to be no consensus regarding the question of whether emotion is more important than reasoning in moral judgments. According to some researchers (see Haidt, 2001; Haidt & Greene, 2002), the emotional reactions of people predominantly drive the process of moral decisions, whereas reasoning is usually insignificant or plays a minor role in the decisions. However, it is not very convincing to other psychologists who view the nature of the relationship between emotion and cognition as reciprocal and inseparable (see Smetana, 2006). Thus, I would like to evaluate the various theories and experiments on the relationship between and roles of emotion and reasoning in moral judgments in this chapter.

First, I will review the theory of Piaget on the relationship between intelligence and affection. As the studies of morality from a cognitive developmental perspective have evolved from the pioneering works of Piaget (1932), it is important to establish basic ideas on this issue from his book *Intelligence and affectivity: Their relationship during child development* (1954). Secondly, I will examine some of the principal psychological studies on the relationship between emotion and cognition. Zajonc (1984) and Lazarus (1984) demonstrated two contrasting ideas on this issue. Their debates are worth exploring to lay a stepping stone for the discussion of moral emotions. Thirdly, I will deal with the arguments over the primacy of emotion in moral judgments. I will analyze how significant and valid they are. Fourthly, I will discuss the results of the neuroimaging studies of Greene and his colleagues (2004) with moral dilemmas. It is exciting to adopt high technologies such as fMRI for the studies of morality and to clarify the implications of these experiments. Lastly, I will share my ideas regarding the formation of an integrated perspective on the roles of emotion and cognition in the studies of moral judgments.

Piagetian Assumptions on the Relationship between Cognition and Emotion

Piaget (1950) suggested that emotion and cognition are inseparable in any human mental activities: "No affect can exist without a minimum of understanding or discrimination" (p. 5). In other words, all human behaviors are composed of both intellect and affect (Piaget, 1954). For example, a young girl follows the instruction not to fight with friends with both a sense of respect for others and a comprehension of this rule. Even basic instinctual behaviors include both rudimentary sentiments and sensorimotor schemata (e.g., the intelligence constructed out of reflexes). For instance, an infant's instinct for eating is composed of reflexes such as sucking as well as emotional reactions such as a desire to be fed. From the Piagetian view, emotion and cognition function together in every human behavior from birth to death.

Then, Piaget (1950, 1966) tried to explain the distinctive roles of cognition and emotion without disrupting his main premise of the inseparable relationship between cognition and emotion. On the one hand, emotion plays a role as an energizing force in human psychological operations. It motivates and drives all intellectual activities. On the other hand, intelligence generates cognitive structures, such as math rules, grammar, syllogisms, and classification, which make mental operations take place in coherent patterns. In a figurative manner, emotion and cognition in a human action can be compared to the fuel and engine in a vehicle (Piaget, 1954): The former stimulates and accelerates one's mental and/or physical action just as the fuel activates a vehicle, whereas the latter selects and applies cognitive structures to situations as the engine moves the vehicle on the street. As the fuel and engine of a vehicle cannot be dissociated in its movement while performing unique functions, emotion and cognition are neither separable nor interchangeable in any human behaviors.

In terms of emotional development, Piaget (1954) suggested that some emotions eventually have structures like intelligence. In the early stages of child development, emotions do not share the mental structures which cognition generates. In the later stages (i.e., from 8 to 12 years of age), however, some emotions such as moral feelings are equipped with the structures which are transferred from intelligence. For example, mutual respect is considered to be an emotion with a structure, as it possesses consistency and reciprocity like a mature moral judgment. Individuals with this affective structure acknowledge in a consistent manner that both they and their friends deserve due respect and that all of them contribute to the effective functioning of group activities. Instead, infants and toddlers mainly reveal spontaneous feelings or intuitive sentiments that last for a moment with reference to a specific object, because they do not have a higher system which governs diverse schemata in relation to each other (Piaget, 1968; see Ginsburg & Opper, 1988). Eventually, young children acquire consistent feelings toward certain objects such as unilateral respect for parents. Their feelings are as yet neither shared nor reciprocal in their interactions with others. Due to these limitations, infants and young children are not considered to have affective structures. In later stages, emotion can possess coherent and objective qualities in an independent manner due to the advanced quality of mental structures, which regulate and integrate various cognitive schemata and emotional reactions in a harmonious manner.

As Piaget did not conduct many empirical studies on the emotional development of children, his ideas on emotions should be adopted with scrutiny. For instance, Piaget found that children have the sense of mutual respect from about eight years of age. But some may argue that children experience mutual respect earlier than Piaget expected. This kind of controversy needs to be verified by empirical studies. Therefore, I would like to apply only two main premises of Piaget to the review of the studies on relationship between cognition and emotion in moral judgments. The first premise is that both moral emotion and reasoning interact inseparably in and contribute to moral judgments; as Piaget suggests, emotion and cognition cannot be dissociated in human judgments and behaviors. The second premise is that moral emotions can be conceptualized to have consistent mental structures. If all sorts of emotional reactions simply represent the strength of motivation or the temporary mood of an individual, it may not be logical to entitle a type of emotion as moral. The idea of the presence of mental structures in certain emotions makes it possible to acknowledge certain types of emotion as moral in a stable and objective manner. These two main premises of Piaget become guiding principles to evaluate the studies regarding the integration of emotion and cognition in general as well as in moral development.

Explanation of Relationship between Emotion and Cognition

Izard et al. (1984) acknowledged that the clarification of the relationship between cognition and emotion in human development is one of the greatest challenges in psychology. This challenge was brought up in a debate over the primacy of emotion or cognition. Some psychologists, such as Izard (1984, 1986; see Ackerman et al., 1988) and Zajonc (1984), supported the primacy of emotion, whereas other researchers, such as Lazarus (1984, 1991a, 1991b) and Mandler (1982), maintained the primacy of cognition. These two different streams of thought also gave rise to opposite views in the psychological underpinnings of emotional development. The former suggested that emotional processes are basically based on neurophysiological and biological functions of the human body. The latter maintained that emotion is developed and regulated by cognition. By reviewing this debate, I hope to find a bridge between the premises of Piaget and the empirical studies on the roles of emotion and reasoning in moral judgments.

Emotion without or with Cognition

Zajonc (1984) viewed cognition and emotion as two separate systems in development and maintained that emotional processes can be activated without cognitive mediation. Along the same line, Ackerman et al. (1998) also refuted the necessity of cognition in some emotional processes and held that the emotional reactions derive directly from the activity of the neurochemical substrates. They maintained that a pure sensory input, which is not part of cognition, can evoke some emotional experiences. For example, a frog shifts its attention from a lily pad to a snake without the perception of the snake itself. The stimulus that moves the frog's attention is an explicit form of change in the environment, that is a variation in the ripple patterns of the water. This kind of sensorimotor activation, which radically influences emotion, involves no cognitive activity because it "needs not to be transformed into meaningful information" (Zajonc, 1984, p. 121). In this approach, the presence of the two independent and separate neuroanatomical structures for emotion and cognition is assumed. In general, these two structures are interactive in various ways in a human organism. However, they can be disconnected in unconsciously or subconsciously motivated behaviors like reflexes. It happens since they are basically two separate systems. In this relationship, emotions can predetermine the contents and directions of behaviors prior to cognitive awareness.

In contrast, Lazarus (1984, 1991a, 1991b) maintained that appraisal, as a type of cognitive activity, is necessary for emotional experience. According to him, "Appraisal consists of a continuing evaluation of the significance of what is happening for one's personal being" (Lazarus, 1991a, p. 144). Individuals cannot have an emotion without an evaluation of a change in their relationship with environment, whether social or physical. In his theory, cognitive activities precede emotional experiences. Lazarus (1984, 1990) did not focus on the neural basis of emotion and cognition but restricted the definition of emotion to the realm of psychophysiological phenomena and distinguished it from simple physiological responses such as neurological reactions over certain sensory inputs, such as noxious odors and tastes. Thus, Lazarus constructed his theory about the primacy between emotion and cognition with a different premise of the physiological underpinnings of emotion and cognition from that of Zajonc. As he viewed that simple reflexes or physiological arousal without appraisal would not be classified as emotions, his understanding of emotion was not the same as that of Zajonc (1984).

In a similar way to Lazarus, Mandler (1982) made a distinction between physiological arousal and emotions by suggesting that cognitive activity and autonomic nervous system (ANS) arousal construct emotional experience. An ANS feedback with no cognitive mediation is not emotion, but remains as physiological arousal. This feedback needs another main condition for the formation of emotion, which is cognition. Although Lazarus and Mandler adopted different terminologies for the necessary cognitive activity for emotional experience, both of them supported the primacy of cognition in its relationship with emotion.

The Issue of Definition in the Debate over the Primacy of Emotion or Cognition

In the debate between Zajonc (1984) and Lazarus (1984) over the primacy of emotion or cognition, definitions of cognition and emotion were raised as one of the main issues. Both agreed that no emotional reaction is possible without stimuli, information, or input. Zajonc (1984) separated cognition from purely sensory inputs, while criticizing Lazarus for not specifying distinctions between cognition, perception, and sensation and for creating a theory only with definitions, i.e., without evidence. Then, he maintained that it is premature to define cognitive aspects of emotional experiences without substantial empirical data and evidence. While I agree with Zajonc that a theory needs empirical evidence, I find that his delay in defining cognition is logically problematic. How could he maintain that emotion precedes cognition without defining cognition? How could he suggest that perception does not belong to cognition without clarifying the nature of cognition? Surely, many definitions are imperfect and modifiable. Nonetheless, psychological theories and studies without definitions may not be valid.

Lazarus (1984) believed that definitions are "an integral part of a theory that helps delimit the phenomena of interest and organize observations" (p. 124). Certainly, the design of a scientific study and the interpretation of empirical data on the relationship between emotion and cognition rely on the definitions of basic concepts. When the definition of cognition includes various levels of information-processing, including sensorimotor activities and perceptions (Piaget, 1950), researchers are not able to find any emotional experiences without cognitive mediation. In contrast, if the definition of cognition does not include certain perceptions (Ackerman et al., 1998), it will be possible to find some emotional states which are not influenced by cognitive appraisal or reasoning. Thus, the issue of the definitions of emotion and cognition should not be treated as an unnecessary component of the research in this field.

The Confirmation of the Inseparability of Emotion and Cognition

My main concern does not lie in the primacy of emotion or cognition, but in finding a theory of emotion which is compatible with the idea of Piaget on the inseparability of emotion and cognition. When emotion and cognition are considered to be two separate structures which govern human behaviors and mental activities in different manners, the danger of duality or dichotomy becomes great. From a dichotomy, researchers would not be able to build up a theoretical framework on which the reasoning and emotional experience of people can interact in and contribute to a decision-making process without excluding the active roles of either emotion or cognition. Furthermore, the researchers with a dichotomous view are more likely to seek the presence of the two different neural systems of the human brain and suggest the primacy of emotion over cognition, maintaining that emotional reactions are associated with the primitive parts of the brain as the result of early evolution. In fact, this tendency has been found in many fields from sociobiology (Wilson, 1975, 1978, 2005) to neuroscience (Greene et al., 2001; Greene et al., 2004).

Lazarus (1984, 1991a) criticized neuroscientific studies for using evidence of activity in different areas of the brain to designate emotion and cognition as separate phenomena. When cognition and emotion are construed as independent, emotional reactions tend to be regarded as biological phenomena which do not include cognitive activities. In the field of psychology, Izard and Zajonc posited a neurological basis for emotion. Before them, James, Lange, Freud, and Herbart had already interpreted emotion as a biological phenomenon (Brown & Kozak, 1988). Other psychologists with neuroscientific approaches have also attempted to reduce emotions to neurological phenomena. For example, Panksepp et al. (1988) proposed that emotions were associated with separable neural circuits located in the subcortical area of the brain. Those researchers tend to think that biological needs or physiological conditions induce emotions and emotions then cause intellectual activities. From those perspectives, the intellectual capacity of human beings does not consistently take an active role in decision-making processes and is frequently controlled by biological and environmental conditions. In contrast, Lazarus and other researchers have proposed that emotion and cognition are inseparable in normal behaviors and developmental states (see Arsenio & Lover, 1995; Griffin & Mascolo, 1998; Piaget, 1950, 1954). Their views are compatible with the theories of moral development which regard children as active intelligent agents of moral judgments, such as the stage theory of Kohlberg (1969) and the domain theory of Turiel (1983).

The Primacy of Emotion in the Dual Process of Moral Judgment

The debate over the primacy of emotion or reasoning is present in the study of moral judgment. Greene, Haidt, and their colleagues (Greene & Haidt, 2002; Greene et al., 2004; Greene et al.,

2008; Haidt, 2001) devised the dual process theory of moral judgment in an effort to integrate traditional theories of moral development and recent moral theories. They maintained that the former focus on the role of reason, whereas the latter emphasize the role of emotion and intuition. Greene et al. (2004) further suggested that there has been a tension between utilitarianism and deontology in the history of moral philosophy. In the former, morality is a matter of achieving the greatest good for the greatest number of people, whereas, in the latter, morality is a matter of obeying rules and fulfilling duties. In the dual process theory, they transformed these two different philosophical approaches into two independent processes of moral judgments; the utilitarian and deontological (or non-utilitarian) judgments. They proposed that cognitive control and abstract reasoning play main roles in utilitarian moral judgments, whereas automatic emotional responses lead to deontological judgments. The former judgments tend to be slow, effortful, and conscious, whereas the latter, fast, easy, and automatic. Of the two processes, the automatic emotional processes (i.e., deontological judgments) tend to be dominant in moral decisions (Greene & Haidt, 2002).

Greene and his colleagues (Greene et al., 2001; Greene et al., 2004) conducted functional magnetic resonance imaging (fMRI) studies of the brain activity of participants and support the dual process theory of moral judgment with the results from these studies. For their experiments, they adopted two types of moral dilemma; impersonal and personal. A typical moral-impersonal dilemma was the trolley dilemma. A trolley is heading toward five workers who work on a track. It will hit and kill them unless the direction of the trolley is changed to another track on which only one person stands. In this situation, participants should decide whether it is appropriate to control the switch to change the direction of the trolley to save the five and kill the one. This dilemma was considered as "impersonal" mainly because the actor is not involved in causing a direct harm to another person.

Instead, a typical moral-personal dilemma in the study of Green et al. (2001) was the footbridge dilemma. In this scenario, the protagonist stands on a footbridge together with a stranger who is physically big. Under the footbridge, a trolley is heading toward five people on a track and about to hit and kill them. The only way to stop the trolley is to push the stranger off the bridge onto the track because his big body can prevent it from moving further. The stranger will surely die. Participants should answer whether it is appropriate to sacrifice the life of the stranger to save the five. This dilemma was considered as "personal" because the actor in the scenario directly inflicts harm on another person to help other people.

According to Greene et al. (2001), the personal dilemma tends to provoke strong emotional reactions.

> The thought of pushing someone to his death is, we propose, more emotionally salient than the thought of hitting a switch that will cause a trolley to produce similar consequences, and it is this emotional response that accounts for people's tendency to treat these cases differently. (p. 2106)

After they assumed that the difference between the trolley dilemma and the footbridge dilemma lies in the variations in the level of emotional involvement, they tried to prove it by analyzing the physiological reactions of the participants when they decided whether to kill one to save five in the two situations.

The results of the study consist in two parts: the images of the activities of brain by fMRI and the length of time that a participant spends in responding to a dilemma (i.e., reaction time: RT). First, the regions of the brain involved in emotional processing were more active in the moral-personal situation (e.g., footbridge dilemma) than in the moral-impersonal condition (e.g., trolley dilemma). Medial prefrontal cortex, posterior cingulate/precuneus, and superior temporal sulcus/temporoparietal junction were the brain areas whose activities increased in the moral-personal circumstances. Secondly, significant differences in the RT (reaction time) were found in the moral-personal dilemmas. The responses of "appropriate" (i.e., kill one to save five in the footbridge dilemma) were slower than those of "inappropriate" (i.e., not to kill one to save five). The possible explanations for these two results were more or less the same. On the one hand, the personal dilemmas were more emotionally salient and demanding than the impersonal. On the other hand, the responses of "inappropriate" in the personal dilemmas (i.e., not pushing a man) created greater emotional reactions, which induced fast decisions, than those of "appropriate" (i.e., pushing a man). Emotional factors, thus, distinguished the types of dilemma as well as the responses to the moral-personal dilemmas. From these analyses, Greene and Haidt (2002) argued that the role of reasoning tends to be limited in moral decision-making processes and that automatic emotional reactions tend to dominate the processes.

A Problematic Distinction between Utilitarian and Deontological Judgments

Among the two types of dilemma, Greene and his colleagues (2004) mainly analyzed the binary responses of participants to moral-personal dilemmas. Because the moral-personal dilemmas (e.g., footbridge dilemma) tend to create a high level of internal conflict in the decision-making process of participants, they are likely to induce both utilitarian and deontological judgments and to become useful for the verification of the dual process of morality. In this analysis, the answer "appropriate" to kill one instead of five in the personal dilemmas becomes utilitarian, whereas the answer "inappropriate" becomes deontological. The former is driven by abstract reasoning and cognitive control which take into account the consequences of their decisions, i.e., a question of whether the judgments maximize collective benefits, whereas the latter is regulated by automatic emotional responses with a simple consideration of moral obligations.

It is noted that the cognitive control of utilitarian judgments implies conflict between reason and emotion. The thought of harming another person creates strong aversive emotional reactions, but they should be controlled by cognition in order to save more persons. Interestingly, Greene et al. (2004) did not assume in a serious manner the presence of similar conflicts in the deontological judgments of moral-personal dilemmas, even though these judgments could be made through the evaluation of both possibilities (i.e., "not to kill one but to let the five die" or "to kill one to save the five"). The participants who judged not to push a big stranger off the footbridge might hardly forget that their judgments made five workers die. Cognitive processes in their mind probably included more than a type of simple, decisive thought such as "I should not kill another person." It is, thus, quite certain that these deontological judgments could include the cognitive control and the cognitive calculation of consequences as in the utilitarian judgments. Nevertheless, the researchers entered into a discussion on the variations of the speed of decisions with the assumption that one type of decision would be slower than the other type, instead of carrying out a depth analysis of the cognitive process of the participants in their experiments.

Haidt (2001) insisted that moral reasoning is a relatively slow and deliberative process which includes abstract and introspective aspects of thinking unlike moral emotional reactions. This assumption becomes one of the main reasons to support the dual process of moral judgment and verify it by measuring the difference of the velocities of judgments.[3] Thus, variations in the reaction times (RTs) of the responses to moral-personal dilemmas are supposed to be associated with the types of judgments (Greene et al., 2004). The utilitarian judgments which entail moral reasoning (e.g., affirmative responses to sacrifice one to save five) are assumed to be slower than the deontological judgments which entail moral emotion and intuition

---

[3] Haidt (2001, 2003, 2007) proposed the contrast between intuition and reasoning for the support of the dual process model of moral judgment (or social intuitionist model in the articles of Haidt). The intuition in his theory is part of a rapid and automatic process of decision-making and distinct from a slow and deliberate process of reasoning.

(i.e., negative responses). This assumption about the speed of moral judgement becomes a reason to support the primacy of emotion in moral judgments.

Many psychologists and philosophers have criticized the studies and theories of Greene and Haidt (see Kahane, 2012; McGuire et al., 2009). Above all, the theoretical frame of these empirical studies is questionable. It seems to be premature and even illogical to differentiate the two philosophical ways of reasoning according to simple binary responses without having any qualitative analyses of the reasons for the responses of the participants. Nevertheless, Greene et al. (2004) decided that the underlying reasoning of the response "appropriate" was utilitarianism, whereas that of "inappropriate" was deontology. All the participants choosing the same response were believed to have the same way of judging, even though Greene and his colleagues (Greene et al., 2001; Greene et al., 2004) did not interview the participants asking why they chose one of the two options.

As Killen and Smetana (2008) suggested, it is crucial to understand the motivation and intention of the actor, the features of the objects of actions, and the environment of the actor in moral judgments. Without the comprehension of these components of moral decision, there could be no ways to verify if the underlying logics of the affirmative or negative responses of participants are really utilitarian or deontological. The quantitative methods of the neuroimaging studies with complex moral dilemmas should be combined with the qualitative studies of moral development. In addition, it is doubtful that philosophical terms such as deontology and utilitarianism are adopted with a correct understanding of their implications and truly represent the essential features of the judgments of people in these studies with moral dilemmas (see Kahane, 2015; Kahane et al., 2018; Rosas & Koenigs, 2014).

Questions about the Analysis of Reaction Times

The variations in the reaction times (RTs) were considered as an empirical base for the dual process theory with an assumption of quick deontological and slow utilitarian judgments. Although Greene et al. (2001) declared that they found the evidence for the variations, other studies raised many doubts and found some results to contradict their evidence. McGuire et al. (2009) analyzed the data of Greene et al.'s studies in 2001 with different methods. For example, nine items of the 40 moral dilemmas that Greene et al. (2001) adopted revealed low rates of affirmative response (e.g., it is appropriate to kill one person to save five). Less than 5% of the participants chose the option "appropriate" as a response to those nine items. They were categorized as 'poorly endorsed items' and excluded from the analysis of the RTs. In that analysis, the RT of response "appropriate" was not significantly different from that of "inappropriate" in the moral-personal dilemmas. It denoted that deontological judgements were not faster than utilitarian judgments. In other words, the automatic emotional reaction was not faster than the judgment with cognitive control and abstract reasoning. This contradicting result demonstrated the truth of Greene et al.'s study in 2001, i.e., the differences in the RTs of responses were mainly influenced by the small number of "poorly endorsed items." In the end, McGuire et al. (2009) concluded that they could not find any data to support the dual process theory of moral judgment. When there were no significant differences in the reaction time between the utilitarian and deontological judgments, the classification of the responses by these philosophical terms and the assumptions about fast emotional reaction and slow moral reasoning became groundless and invalid.

Greene et al. (2008) acknowledged the need for a significant transformation of their dual process theory in order to explain the unexpected results, and even suggested the possibility that "utilitarian normative principles are more consciously accessible than competing deontological principles, and that they are therefore more easily routinized into a decision procedure" (p. 1152). This interpretation that people can do quick moral reasoning is a serious challenge to their theory. Since no differences were found in the RTs between the two judgments, the two types of judgments were different from each other only by apparent responses, i.e., one is "appropriate," and the other is "inappropriate." Then, it became uncertain whether the affirmative response is really utilitarian (i.e., driven mainly by moral reasoning). In the same vein, no data help understand whether the negative response is truly deontological (i.e., driven by emotional reactions).

Complications in the Interpretation of Neuroimaging Studies

Greene et al. (2004) attempted to prove the distinction between the utilitarian and deontological judgments with the analysis of fMRI images of brain activities. One of the findings of the study confirmed that the utilitarian judgments of moral-personal dilemmas showed increased activities in the dorsolateral prefrontal cortex (DLPFC) over the deontological judgments. DLPFC is known for the function of cognitive control. Thus, it may be suggested that the utilitarian judgment of moral-personal dilemma (i.e., it is "appropriate" to harm one to save several persons) consists of a higher level of cognitive control than the deontological one which is rather emotional than rational. If this kind of idea is valid, the dual process theory of moral judgment may find some evidence. Nevertheless, the results of neuroimaging studies and their implications have not been straightforward. Even some contradictory results have been observed in the studies of Koenigs and his colleagues (see Koenigs et al., 2007; Koenigs & Tranel, 2007).

Koenigs et al. (2007) assumed that patients with damage to the ventral medial prefrontal cortex (VMPFC) of the brain were more likely to make a utilitarian judgment, which was rather rational than emotional, because the lesion of VMPFC was known to cause emotional deficits. The results of their study confirmed it: The patients with emotional deficits due to VMPFC lesions made approximately five times more utilitarian judgments than the participants in the control groups in moral-personal dilemmas such as the footbridge dilemma. As the patients made much less deontological judgments, which were considered to be emotive and intuitive, it was assumed that the emotional deficits due to the lesion may make them experience less aversive feelings and use more cognitive functions such as reasoning and calculation than healthy people. Seemingly, this result supports the minor role of emotion, which prevents one from harming another person, in the utilitarian judgment and its major role in the deontological judgment. Subsequently, it may become a base for the dual process theory of moral judgments which emphasize the differentiated emotional reactions by the types of judgment, if it is consistently found in other studies.

By contrast, another study of Koenig and his colleague did not reveal similar results such as the positive association between the frequency of utilitarian judgment and the lack of the activities of the brain regions related to emotions (Koenigs & Tranel, 2007, see Talmi & Frith, 2007; Rosas & Koenigs, 2014). Unlike the study of Koenigs et al. (2007), Koenigs and Tranel (2007) found that these patients make irrational judgments against the principle of utilitarianism. They used the ultimatum game for studies with the patients with the VMPFC lesion. In the game of two persons, a proposer of the experiment offers to share $10 with a participant in various ratios such as 5:5 and 1:9. The participant decides whether to accept the offer of the proposer. The acceptance means to gain the portion of money which the proposer suggests, whereas the rejection, to gain no money. By accepting the offers, a participant can make his or her benefits increase (i.e., utilitarian decision). However, certain offers do not look fair to participants. For instance, it may be viewed as fair that the proposer gives $5 to the participant and keeps $5, whereas it may be viewed as unfair that the proposer gives $1 and keeps $9. Since the participant gains money even with seemingly unfair offers, it is assumed as utilitarian or rational to accept any offers. According to the results of this study, the VMPFC patients demonstrated a higher rate of rejection than the participants in comparison groups for unfair offers. It implies that the judgments of the patients were driven by emotional reactions such as anger more than cognitive calculations.

The results of the studies with the VMPFC patients are paradoxical as they mainly made rational decisions (i.e., utilitarian) in one situation and irrational or emotional decisions (i.e., deontological) in the other (Talmi & Frith, 2007). These outwardly contradictory results suggest the complexity of the human mind and the limitations of neuroimaging studies. As the human brain and mind are closely associated, it is possible to study the brain substrates of decision-making processes. However, it is clear that the presence of the link between an intricate judgment and a single part of the brain is illusory. Moreover, as the same decision of individuals can be triggered by varying emotions and made for different reasons, there is no guarantee that apparently similar judgments and reactions are associated with the same neural substrates of the brain.

In a way, the paradox of the studies with the patients with a brain lesion may indicate that neuroimaging studies on brain and mind should not fall into the errors of phrenology in the past. Phrenology is based on the assumption that "the mind is composed of a finite number of mental faculties all located in some particular area of the brain and detectable by feeling the bumps on the head." (Schaffer, 2006, p. 61). This sort of belief that the specific parts of the brain are responsible for certain emotions and thoughts is better not to revive in contemporary studies. Damasio (2003) addressed this issue as follows: "In spite of the major importance of certain regions in the unfolding of this or that phenomenon, the processes of mind and behavior result from the concerted operation of the *many* regions that constitute brain systems, small and large" (p. 308). Advanced technologies such as fMRI enable scientists to examine some correlates of brain function during specific human operations. Most of them do not pursue phrenological analyses, because a single part of the human brain cannot be responsible for the complex functions of humans such as moral judgments. Thus, the readers of neuroimaging studies on morals should review and interpret the results on the neuroanatomical correlates of human function, having in mind the complex nature of the link between brain functions and human judgments.

A New Interpretation of the Data of Patients with VMPFC Damage

Eventually, Rosas and Koenigs (2014) suggested a different way to analyze the data that Koenigs and his colleagues found in the past (Koenigs et al., 2007; Koenigs et al., 2012). Adopting the approach of Choe and Min (2011), they classified moral-personal dilemmas into categories based on principal emotional reactions. For instance, the footbridge dilemma belongs to a category which does not include any extra aspects that intensify the level of anger, sadness, or guilt (Rosas & Koenigs, 2014). For this group of dilemmas, the patients with VMPFC damage did not make significantly more utilitarian judgments than healthy participants. Even though it was known that they made five times more utilitarian judgments than others in the previous analysis of Koenigs et al. (2007), the re-analysis revealed a contrasting result in the tests of the group of scenarios including the footbridge dilemma. Thus, Rosas and Koenigs (2014) confirmed that the opinion about the bias of VMPFC patients toward utilitarian judgments (see Greene et al., 2008) does not respond correctly to the actual tendency of the patients.

In general, the new analysis and findings of Rosa and Koenigs (2014) can provide different possibilities to view the role of emotion in moral reasoning and decision and the association between brain areas and the types of judgments. Specifically, they made a suggestion which changes the paradigm of the dual process of moral judgment. According to them, "The endorsement of personal harms in these clinical groups appears to be based more on sensitivity (or insensitivity) to particular social-affective factors that vary across scenarios within this set of stimuli, rather than on a strictly utilitarian mindset" (Rosas & Koenigs, 2014, p. 665). Thus, it is no longer correct to maintain that the patients with VMPFC lesions make a judgment to sacrifice one to save others, which was considered as utilitarian, because they are not bothered by aversive emotions.

Various Roles of a Brain Region

The functions of a brain region should be understood more profoundly and broadly in order to analyze correctly the data of neuroimaging studies. For an example from the neuroimaging studies on morality, DLPFC (i.e., dorsolateral prefrontal cortex) was mainly known for cognition related activities (see Greene et al., 2004), whereas VMPFC (i.e., ventral medial prefrontal cortex) of the brain was considered to be involved mainly in emotional reactions (see Greene et al., 2008; Koenigs et al., 2007). As the findings of scientific studies are accumulated and systematized, refined comprehensions of the functions of particular area(s) in the brain have been produced. It is now known that brain regions are involved in a variety of functions.

Particularly, Hiser and Koenigs (2017) succinctly explained the various roles of VMPFC regarding decision making, social cognition, and emotional reaction by analyzing the results of various empirical studies. The VMPFC plays a critical role not only in "the generation and regulation of negative emotion" but also in "the representation of reward- and value-based decision making" and in "multiple aspects of social cognition" (Hiser & Koenigs, 2017, p. 638). These roles of VMPFC evolve not as its independent project but as a cooperation with other parts of the brain. These configurations of cooperative groups vary by the functions. In the studies of moral development, thus, our understanding of brain functions for moral judgments and behaviors can develop when researchers with neuroimaging methods are able to design their experiments based on their comprehension of the multifaceted roles of brain regions.

Toward an Integrated View on Emotion and Cognition in Moral Judgments

In a process of moral judgment, individuals try to integrate emotional reactions and rational considerations for a right decision. After I have critically reviewed Greene et al.'s empirical studies (Greene et al., 2004; Greene et al., 2008) and other studies based on neuroimaging data (Hiser & Koenigs, 2017; Koenigs & Tranel, 2007; Koenigs et al., 2007; Rosas & Koenigs, 2014), I suggest that the binary classification of moral judgments such as emotional and rational (or deontological and utilitarian) is neither logically valid nor scientifically informative from a cognitive developmental perspective. Above all, the premise of Piaget (1954)—the inseparability of emotion and reasoning—logically invalidates the primacy of emotion or cognition in moral judgment. All judgments have to include both emotional and cognitive components. Neither rationality nor affect alone can induce a moral decision. Furthermore, Kohlberg (1969, 1971, 1981), unlike the approach of Greene and his colleagues, did not evaluate the qualities of the moral judgments of individuals by classifying their binary responses to questions regarding dilemmas but by analyzing the logical grounds of the responses. As he knew that the simple answer of "Yes" or "No" could not reveal the internal dimension of judgment, Kohlberg examined justifications for response, the process of decision-making, and the formal features of judgment in order to explicate in what types of reasoning individuals engage and how they discuss various aspects concerning moral dilemmas. Therefore, it may not be feasible to utilize or analyze the empirical data of Greene and his colleagues in a productive way without the transformation of core assumptions of their theory and adopting some solid premises and methods for the examination of the underlying cognitive schemata and emotional processes of moral judgments.

Morality has been one of the important themes in the long tradition of philosophical studies. Thus, many psychologists and neuroscientists who study this theme have adopted the philosophical terms and insights regarding human morals. In this process, it is crucial for them to respect, understand, and apply the ideas of philosophers without distortion. According to Kahane and his colleagues (2012; Kahane et al., 2015; Kahane et al., 2018), the utilitarian judgments which allow the sacrifice of an innocent person in the hypothetical moral dilemmas in the studies of Greene and his colleagues do not reflect the genuine ideas of a utilitarian approach to morality such as the presence of impartiality in maximization of the well-being of individuals. It implies that utilitarian judgments differ from the simple decision that it is better to save five persons instead of one. Furthermore, unlike the suggestion of Greene and his colleagues (Greene & Haidt, 2002; Greene et al., 2004; Greene et al., 2008) that deontological judgments are primarily associated with emotions and intuitions, Kantian traditions indicate that moral decisions include abstract thinking as they take place with the conscious awareness of ethical principles and prescriptive standards (see Kant, 1785; Williams, 2018). Even though Kant acknowledged the importance of moral emotions, he would be perplexed if his deontology was perceived as an emotion-ridden approach. Therefore, the approach of Greene and his colleagues seems to be misguided, because it identified the utilitarian and deontological judgments as rational and emotional decisions, respectively. Certainly, it is useful to combine philosophical concepts with an empirical approach to morality. When psychologists and other researchers go beyond the boundaries of their own disciplines, however, they should acknowledge that they can only understand and illustrate human morality by learning the perspectives of scholars in philosophy and other fields, not simply by borrowing the terminologies of others.

From a cognitive developmental perspective, humans are not passive beings whose decisions are automatically regulated by certain stimuli from the environment or neural substrates of the brain, but active agents who can make moral judgments by considering both rational and emotional factors in their interactions with social and physical environments (see Kohlberg, 1968; Turiel, 2002). This vision of human beings prevents psychologists from falling into reductionism, i.e., reducing the complex phenomena of the human psyche to simple elements. For instance, the idea of the primacy of emotion over cognition in moral judgment implies that individuals tend to judge according to emotional reactions rather than reasoning (Greene, 2009; Greene et al., 2001; Haidt, 2001, 2003, 2007). In this understanding of morality, reasoning tends to be secondary or epiphenomenal, compared to emotion, in critical moral judgments and the nature of these moral judgments seems to be reduced to an emotional reaction. To avoid an objectionable reductionism, thus, it is essential to maintain an integrated perspective on humans whose intelligence and affect are consistently united in their moral decisions and actions. In addition, I do acknowledge that neuroscience has contributed remarkably to the understanding of human behaviors and will bring about significant progress in the studies of morality in the future. Although this science alone cannot fully elucidate human judgments of right and wrong, it can provide a scientific understanding of relevant aspects of moral development such as empathy-related reactions, psychopathological behaviors, and age-related changes in the brain (see Malti & Ongley, 2013). Hopefully, many psychologists and neuroscientists share an integrated vision of moral development and cooperate in order to reach new insights about the interaction between emotion and cognition in moral reasoning and decision.

4

Do Children Differentiate Morality from Convention?

Researcher: If everybody in another country decided to play football by different rules than we do here, would that be all right?

Charles (6 years, 10 month): Yes. Our way here is the way we have here and if they have a different way they could make it their way.

Researcher: Let's say that all the people in another country decided that in their country it's all right to steal. So they didn't have any rules or laws about it: Do you think it would be right?

Jim (7 years, 1 month): No . . . because some people wouldn't like to have things stolen. (Turiel, 1983, pp. 83−85)

Charles did not mind that people in another country had different rules for football games, whereas Jim was concerned about people in another country which did not have a law against stealing. Does this difference in their concerns about people in another country have any implications for moral development? By adopting this type of contrast as a sign of divergence between moral and conventional reasoning, Turiel and his colleagues (1983, 2002; Smetana, 2006) opened a new way to comprehend the nature of moral development.

The rational capacity of humans to evaluate the necessity of rules and to modify the laws of society goes beyond their concerns about their own country. They can make a judgment about rules and laws in other nations. Like in the examples, children may believe that people in other countries can have their own unique rules for games and sports, whereas they may think the law against theft is essential to protect the properties of people in every country. In other words, some rules can be decided by a local community, whereas others should be applied to all of humanity. In the context of social reasoning, the former represents convention, whereas the latter represents morality. The age of children to make this distinction is closely related to the development of Turiel's social domain theory (1983). In this chapter, I will review and discuss the basic ideas of his theory

First, I will explain how Turiel (1983) found that children conceptualize different systems of social reasoning such as moral and conventional domains. The former is based on social ideals such as social justice and human dignity, whereas the latter is composed of common social rules and regulations for efficient interactions in a society. Turiel suggested that children can differentiate between the two domains of social reasoning in the early stage of development. Secondly, I will review the theories of Piaget and Kohlberg in light of the social domain theory of Turiel in order to discuss the importance of the distinction between morality and convention. Turiel generally agrees with Piaget and Kohlberg regarding a view of human nature and research method. However, his findings on the early emergence of children's capacity for domain distinction resulted in inevitable conflicts with the stage theories of moral development proposed by Piaget and Kohlberg. Thus, in the last part of this chapter, I will discuss the implications of the shift from stage theory to the social domain approach in the studies of moral development, and examine the significance of the distinction between the two domains for the promotion of social justice and human rights.

The Birth of Social Domain Theory

In 1983, Elliot Turiel published his book *The development of social knowledge: Morality and convention.* In this book, he explained systematically his social domain theory. When children experience various interactions with parents, siblings, peers, and other people in a society, they begin to observe varied patterns regarding bases for decision-making, relations with rules or authority, and the consequences of judgments. For example, school-aged children know that they cannot play with their friends until midnight without a special permission from their parents. Instead, they know that it is good and right for them to approach their friends in distress and console them, whether or not their parents or teachers give them a permission to do so. These examples show certain contrasting features in the judgments of children. In some cases, children tend to make their judgments according to the rules and commands which authority figures impose on them, as in the first example. In other cases, they can make their judgments according to their own understanding of the wellness of people and the fair distribution of opportunities and resources, as in the second example. In studies of moral development, the former is known to be a type of conventional reasoning, whereas the latter, moral reasoning. These different sorts of reasoning are grouped as distinct domains in social reasoning. Each domain constitutes a system of thinking with particular bases and formal characteristics. In general, children implicitly use these distinct domains to organize their thoughts and actions and proceed to their judgments and choices (see Smetana, 2006; Turiel, 1983, 2006).

Turiel (1983) presented several empirical studies which demonstrated a distinction between moral and conventional domain in the reasoning of children. Smetana (1981b), one of the pioneering researchers of the social domain theory, investigated whether three- or four-year-old children in the United States could distinguish between moral and conventional transgressions. An example of moral transgressions was the physical violence of a child against another child, and that of conventional transgressions was a failure to put things back to original places after using them. The young participants in the research were asked to evaluate how serious these transgressions were. They thought that moral transgressions were more serious and deserved greater punishment than conventional ones. According to these sorts of experimental findings (Nucci & Turiel, 1978; Smetana, 1981b; Turiel, 1977), the distinction between moral and conventional judgments exists in the reasoning of children of three or four years of age. The discovery of this capacity at an early age by Turiel and his colleagues necessitated the formulation of the domain theory of social reasoning.

The Characteristics of Moral Reasoning

Based on the examination of ethical theories and the analysis of empirical studies, Turiel (1983) explicated the characteristics of moral reasoning and suggested that the moral domain of social reasoning is grounded in the concept of wellbeing, justice, and human rights, and moral judgments are independent of laws or authority and are applicable to all human beings (see Smetana, 2006). The first part of this definition of moral domain deals with justifications for judgments, i.e., the bases or values with which individuals make judgments. They are composed of the wellbeing of individuals (i.e., preserving the physical and mental integrity of human beings from violence or other types of harm), justice (i.e., distributing fairly necessary goods to people), and human rights (i.e., acknowledging the basic human rights of individuals regardless of race, age, and gender). When children are asked why it is wrong to steal the belongings of others, they are likely to justify their judgments with these reasons. On the other hand, the second part of the definition deals with the criteria of moral judgments which reveal the formal characteristics of moral reasoning. They can be described as independence from laws and authority (i.e., not being dependent on nor subjected to the laws or regulations that the authority of a society establishes), generalizability (i.e., being applicable to all human races beyond national or cultural boundaries), and impersonality (i.e., making a judgment about an individual regardless of personal relationship). Children consider moral failures and duties to be judged by universal social values and to be applied to diverse cultural contexts with no exceptions.

Turiel and his colleagues usually conduct interviews with children and adolescents, following the method of Piaget, i.e., a clinical interview (see Turiel, 1983, pp. 21 − 32). "The clinical examination is thus experimental in the sense that the practitioner sets himself a problem, makes hypotheses, adapts the conditions to them and finally controls each hypothesis by testing it against the reactions he stimulates in conversation" (Piaget, 1929, p. 8). Researchers should understand correctly the theory and method of Piaget and be trained well in order to conduct a clinical interview in a consistent, interactive, and creative manner. In general, an interview consists of the presentation of an event or incident, a question of whether a certain judgment or action is right or wrong, a question of why it is right or wrong, and probing questions to examine the formal features of the reasoning.

For example, researchers present to children a violent incident, saying, "Jim hit his friend with his fist in a classroom." And they ask a question, "Is his behavior right or wrong?" Children judge that hitting a friend is wrong (or right). Then, the researchers ask "Why is it wrong (or right) to hit his friend?" to clarify justifications for the judgment. The children may say that hitting a friend is wrong because the friend gets hurt. This justification can be classified as a concern for welfare. Then, probing questions in a hypothetical manner follow for the assessment of the formal characteristics of the judgment. "If Peter hits his friend in a playground, not in the classroom, would it be all right?" If the children say that hitting a friend is wrong in the classroom as well as in the playground, this answer reveals the generalizability of their judgment in a sense that this reasoning is not confined to a specific situation but applicable to various contexts. Another common question deals with the relationship between authority and morality by presenting an imaginary condition. "Is it all right for Peter to hit his friends, if his father told him that it is not bad for Peter to hit his friend from time to time?" When the children respond negatively to this question, it becomes clear that their judgments do not depend on the rules or teachings of authority figures. As researchers confirm the formal criteria of judgments such as generalizability and independence from authority, they can identify the judgment as moral and distinguish it from the non-moral domains of judgments. By conducting clinical interviews in that way, researchers of social domain theory have proved that young children can make a moral judgment.

The Features of the Conventional Domain

The conventional domain of social reasoning consists in the set of common rules and manners that organize and facilitate the ordinary interactions of people and the functions of public and private groups, and judgments in this domain tend to vary by societies and depend on the norms and rules of the communities and institutions to which the subjects of the judgments belong (see Smetana, 2006; Turiel, 1983). The common contents of the conventional domain include social etiquettes, greeting forms, dress codes, local holiday celebrations, religious rituals, game rules, regulations for movement and traffic, etc. In most cases, common justifications for judgments in the conventional domain can be the effective functioning of the group, the maintenance of social order, the preservation of cultural traditions, etc.

For example, a high school has a policy that students should wear a school uniform. The authority of the school may justify this practice, explaining that the uniform is good for the effectiveness of school education, the formation of school identity, and the preservation of school tradition. However, reasons for judgments in the conventional domain of social reasoning are not always objective and universally applicable, but subjective and locally valid. Some schools without any uniforms can pursue the same aims of the practice of other schools with uniforms in different manners such as a unique pedagogy and creative programs. Thus, conventional judgments depend mainly on the preferences and intentions of social groups such as a nation, city, company, school, family, club, etc. In many cases, the specific reasons for decisions do not have any intrinsic values, unlike the reasons for moral judgments such as justice and welfare. Nevertheless, it is necessary for a group of individuals to go through decision-making processes regarding a variety of themes to vitalize and govern the interpersonal gatherings, social activities, and cultural practices of people.

In terms of the formal criteria of judgments, the conventional domain tends to show a sharp contrast with the moral domain. The former is dependent on rules and is variable according to contexts, whereas the latter is independent of rules and is generalizable beyond local boundaries. First, a reference to the established rules of community is a main formal feature of conventional reasoning. Individuals make judgments in the conventional domain in reference to the rules of society. If there are no relevant rules for a given issue, the consensus of group members or the decisions of authority figures are necessary for the judgments in this domain. By contrast, moral judgments are based more fundamentally on the ideas of human rights and social justice than are the actual laws and regulations of society.

Although conventional judgments are necessary for any community or organization to live in a harmonious and effective way, the specific rules which are created by conventional reasoning do not have any particular values in themselves. In an empirical study, many children judged that eating lunch with fingers is not wrong in the absence of the rule to ban it (see Turiel 1983, p. 59). This is an example of conventional reasoning. This example implies that a judgment of right or wrong does not come from actions themselves, but from the established rules of institutions. Thus, actions and incidents related to social conventions and customs could not be judged clearly without the knowledge of relevant social rules or cultural traditions. In contrast, morally relevant actions and incidents such as theft and violence can be judged wrong or right even in the absence of a rule.

Secondly, human reasoning about conventional practices tends to vary by contexts. In other words, the generalizability of judgment in the moral domain of social reasoning is not found in the formal criteria of conventional judgments. For an example of generalizability in moral reasoning, racial discrimination should be judged morally wrong in the U.S. as well as in China. This formal characteristic of morality implies a sense of universality, as moral judgments are not restricted by the boundaries of nations or cultures. Instead, judgments regarding conventions do not have this formal criterion but tend to be variable according to groups such as families and countries. For example, it is common for Koreans, Chinese, and Vietnamese to celebrate a new year according to the lunar calendar. It is one of the most important festivals of these peoples. However, this lunar new year celebration is not universally recognized. Like this example, judgments in the conventional domain reveals a cultural relativity unlike moral judgments. Thus, judgments in the conventional domain of social reasoning vary by cultures and countries and rely on the established norms and regulations of communities, institutions, and governments.

Simultaneous Development of Moral and Conventional Domains

Turiel constructed his core ideas of social development based on a distinction between moral and conventional reasoning in the mind of children. In fact, Piaget (1932) and Kohlberg (1969) had already paid close attention to the similarity and difference between the two sorts of mental operations of children in their judgments on social issues before Turiel (1983) developed his social domain theory. The autonomy and heteronomy of the theory of Piaget correspond respectively to the moral and conventional reasoning of the domain theory, whereas the post-conventional morality and conventional morality of Kohlberg, to the moral and conventional domain of Turiel. Basically, all of them acknowledged the difference between morality and convention and rejected the simplistic legal vision of morality, which maintains that morality consists in obedience to the laws. While Piaget and Kohlberg saw this obedient tendency as an immature or low-level morality, Turiel defined it as conventional thinking. For Piaget and Kohlberg, an authentic moral judgment should transcend the legal vision of morality or conventional morality, as it is guided by the inner principles of a decision-maker and not by the letter of the law. The divergence between mature and immature moralities reveals the main feature of moral development in their theories. For Turiel, the contrast between two types or levels of moralities is represented by the distinction between morality and convention. Despite the use of different terminologies, all of them tried to figure out when and how children begin to distinguish between moral and conventional reasoning.

Piaget, Kohlberg, and Turiel suggested different ideas about the developmental process of moral and conventional reasoning, although they shared many fundamental visions of humans, intelligence, and organism-environment interactions. Piaget implied that children older than eight years of age could distinguish moral reasoning from conventional thinking. Kohlberg said the same of adolescents. But Turiel (1983, 2002) found that young children of three or four years of age were able to do so. Due to the early emergence of the capacity for distinction, it was theorized that children develop moral and conventional reasoning in a simultaneous manner. As these two types of reasoning have contrasting features regarding formal characteristics, such as universal applicability and independence from rules of morality in contrast to cultural relativity and dependence on rules of convention, they have to emerge at the same time in the developmental process of social reasoning. Thus, the idea of the simultaneous development of the two domains contradicts the theories of Piaget and Kohlberg, which suggests that morality grows out of conventional reasoning, and brings about the reevaluation of the stage theories of moral development.

Piaget: Heteronomy and Autonomy

According to Piaget (1932), there are two stages of morality; heteronomy and autonomy. In his mind, the divergence between the two moralities occurs due to the differences in the human understanding concerning the nature of norms and rules. Heteronomy signifies that the system of rules exists outside of individuals, whereas autonomy implies that it is present inside of them. In terms of developmental sequence, heteronomy develops first and autonomy follows. Young children with heteronomy think they should obey the rules of family, school, and neighborhood, as they view them as absolute and even sacred, and believe that they cannot alter the rules which parents, teachers, and other adults have generated. By contrast, older children with autonomy follow rules, based on their conviction of the significance, necessity, and validity of the rules, and understand that they can modify certain rules or generate new rules by mutual consent. Thus, the comprehension of children about the nature of rules in terms of origin and modifiability becomes a main criterion which distinguishes between heteronomy and autonomy.

The contrast between heteronomy and autonomy made by Piaget resounds well with the distinction between convention and morality proposed by Turiel. As the heteronomous morality of Piaget describes the obedient attitudes of children to the existing rules of family and society and their belief of being righteous due to their adherence to the rules, it is equivalent to the conventional reasoning of the social domain theory of Turiel whose core lies in conformity to the norms and indications of authority figures. On the other hand, the characteristics of autonomy corresponds to those of the moral domain, as both Piaget and Turiel view that genuine moral judgments do not depend solely on the existing law of a society but principally on the conscious knowledge of individuals concerning the realities, ideals, and principles of social interactions and regulations. Thus, individuals with autonomous morality, unlike those with heteronomous morality, can make a judgment in the absence of rules and against problematic regulations. Therefore, Piaget explained clearly the importance of the distinction between morality and convention in his theory.

Despite the common emphasis on the difference between morality and convention, Piaget (1932) did not think about the simultaneous development of the two types of reasoning in early childhood as Turiel (1983) did. Basically, Piaget thought that heteronomy should develop before autonomy. One of the reasons for the divergence between Turiel and Piaget could be related to the classification of activities in the studies of morality. Piaget (1932) developed the main structure of his theory by observing mainly children playing a game of marbles and interviewing them on what to think about the rules of the game. He did not question whether the reasoning of children about rules can vary by the types of activities. Although Piaget classified the qualities of rules such as motor, coercive, and rational, he did not consider seriously that children might differentiate the rules of games from those of good conduct or other morally relevant incidents such as stealing and fighting. Instead, Turiel assumed that rules about cleaning and ordering the house or classroom might not share the same features as the regulations of violence or other misdemeanors in the reasoning of children. Because of the lack of classification of social interactions in his studies, Piaget might not be able to capture the capacity to differentiate morality from convention in the reasoning of young children.

Three Types of Rules in the Process of Moral Development

As Piaget's study of moral reasoning originated from his analysis of the children's understanding about rules, it is beneficial to review his ideas on the developmental process of children's conceptions of rules. Piaget (1932) classified three types of rules; motor rule, coercive rule, and rational rule. Although these rules tend to coexist in many types of children's behaviors, it is necessary to conceptualize these three types of rules in order to analyze the developmental process of moral judgments (Piaget, 1932, p. 87). First, the motor rule implies that infants begin to learn the regular patterns of certain behaviors such as sucking the breast of the mother and playing with "baby mobiles" hanging above the crib. The comprehension of repetitive actions and reactions is composed of the consciousness of motor rule. Young children who start to play the game of marbles simply enjoying picking and throwing the marbles without knowing and obeying the rules of games. Thus, the nature of motor rule is not directly related to morality. It can be viewed as amoral and even asocial in some situations, as children with this rule do not really engage in interpersonal activities with a sense of obligation or a feeling of respect.

Do Children Differentiate Morality from Convention?

Along with the application of motor rules, young children from two years of age become conscious of the various rules which parents impose upon them (Piaget, 1932, p. 89). For instance, mothers asked them to eat a meal in a certain manner and avoid watching T.V. till late in the evening. These rules are different from motor rules, because they are evolved in the context of interpersonal relationship. Because these rules are formulated and given by adults or other authority figures to control and constrain the behaviors of children, Piaget (1932) categorized them as coercive rules. These rules represent heteronomy. As children accept, respect, and follow the coercive rules with a belief that these rules possess absolute value, the quality of coercion or constraint tends to be rather a voluntary submission to the given rules. However, this level of consciousness does not include the genuine qualities of moral and democratic systems. Children with the stage of coercive rules tend to mystify the rules without understanding their ultimate purposes and original motives. As they believe that they lack the capacities to present their own opinions about the rules and to discuss them with others in order to draw a new conclusion, they tend to disregard any need to evaluate the significance and validity of existing rules or to formulate new rules for the betterment of activities and systems. Thus, according to Piaget (1932), these coercive rules are valid and significant for children not because of the contents of the rules but because of the tradition of rules or the authority of the transmitters of the rules.

In contrast, rational rules reflect the genuine features of social interactions among individuals who know how to respect others as well as themselves. In terms of the type of morality, the autonomy of children consists in the rational rules. Children about eight years of age or older begin to understand that the rules of games are neither sacred nor inalterable (Piaget, 1932, p. 71). As they are willing to change the rules of their games in order to make them more interesting, the rules that they have inherited from older children or adults no longer possess any transcendent power in the name of tradition. Instead, the value of rules depends on their functions and effects, not on the origin of the rules. With the rational rules, children stop revealing their unilateral respect for adults and older children, but engage in activities with others in the spirit of equality, mutual respect, and reciprocity. When children can discuss whether they will apply the rules of a game to their practices by consenting to them with a comprehension of motives, they are truly participating in social relationships as autonomous agents. According to Piaget (1932), children should participate in this kind of cooperative process of mutual trust for the application and modification of rules in order to develop a mature form of morality. When this development is applied to the level of society, autonomous individuals with rational rules can construct a community of justice by consistently engaging in evaluations of the current systems and mutually consenting to the laws which guarantee their rights and enhance their dignity (see Piaget, 1932, p. 319).

The difference between heteronomy with coercive rules and autonomy with rational rules in the theory of Piaget denotes the contrast between convention and morality. It can be applied to a developmental transition from heteronomy to autonomy in the context of social changes. Piaget (1932) wrote, "... law now emanates from the sovereign people and no longer from the tradition laid down by the Elders. And correlatively with this change, the respective values attaching to custom and the rights of reason come to be practically reversed" (p. 72). In many cases, the oppression of the rights of reason can be caused by the egoistic motives of the powerful figures who earn benefits from traditional practices. In the ideas of Piaget, the ignorance of individuals in society can also lead to a maintaining of the oppression of their own rights by traditional practices. When the individuals with the mentality of coercive rules do not try to delve into the internal frames of their customary practices and comprehend the motives and reasons of the practices, they tend to mystify traditions and voluntarily enslave themselves to them. In front of the individuals with autonomous reasoning, however, a custom loses its transcendent power and turns out to be an object of discussion and modification for the betterment of human welfare. In this way, Piaget (1932) emphasized how the emancipating qualities of autonomous reasoning contributed to the moral development of individuals and the progress of social justice. This achievement of autonomy for social ideals can be viewed as the victory of human rights over oppressive traditions in human history.

Kohlberg: The Three Levels and Six Stages of Morality

Following the clinical interview method of Piaget (1929, 1932), Kohlberg conducted numerous interviews with children and adolescents and analyzed their answers. In his interviews, he presented hypothetical stories of moral conflicts such as the Heinz dilemma[4] to children and evaluated their stage of moral development by analyzing the quality of the responses of the children. From his empirical studies, Kohlberg (1969, 1981) devised the structure of his theory of moral development by analyzing the relationship between morality and convention. Although his theory is rather known for the six stages of moral development, it principally consists of the three levels of morality; pre-conventional, conventional, and post-conventional morality. Simply because each level included two stages, he presented his theory as the six stages of moral development: The pre-conventional level of moral judgments consists of the 1° obedience and punishment orientation stage and the 2° naïve egocentric orientation stage; the conventional level, 3° good-boy

---

[4] "Heinz's wife was dying from a particular type of cancer. Doctors said a new drug might save her. The drug had been discovered by a local chemist, and Heinz tried desperately to buy some, but the chemist was charging ten times the money it cost to make the drug, and this was much more than Heinz could afford. Heinz could only raise half the money, even after help from family and friends. He explained to the chemist that his wife was dying and asked if he could have the drug cheaper or pay the rest of the money later. The chemist refused, saying that he had discovered the drug and was going to make money from it. The husband was desperate to save his wife, so later that night he broke into the chemist's and stole the drug." (Retrieved from https://www.simplypsychology.org/kohlberg.html)

orientation and 4° authority/social order maintaining orientation; the post-conventional level, 5° contractual legalistic orientation and 6° principled orientation (Kohlberg, 1969). Between the three levels and six stages, the former explicitly reveals the importance of the distinction between morality and convention, as Kohlberg defined the three different structures of moral cognition by analyzing the relation between morals and conventions in human judgments.

When Kohlberg's theory is reviewed with a particular focus on the three levels of moral development, it is rather easy to find a continuity between Piaget and Kohlberg. Although Piaget (1932) suggested two stages of morality (i.e., heteronomy and autonomy), he also discussed the presence of the amoral stage governed by motor rules before the emergence of the two types of morality. In the amoral stage, infants and young children enjoy the activities according to their comprehension of the motor rules of physical activities such as kicking a ball and ringing a bell without engaging in social activities as competent players. While this amoral stage is related to motor rules, heteronomy and autonomy are connected to coercive and rational rules, respectively. In terms of the developmental sequence of reasoning, the amoral, heteronomous, and autonomous stages of Piaget correspond respectively to the pre-conventional, conventional, and post-conventional level of Kohlberg. Even though they had different ideas about the time of the emergence of these thinking patterns, the continuity and correspondence between Piaget and Kohlberg is helpful in grasping the core ideas of Kohlberg's stage theory of moral development.

The Three Rules of Piaget and the Three Levels of Kohlberg

Kohlberg (1969, 1981) considered the pre-conventional morality of children about five to eight years of age not genuinely moral. Since this level is based on the fear of punishment, it differs from genuine moral judgments whose emotional origin resides in a sense of respect. In this period, young children are simply conditioned and constrained by punishment and rewards by adults. The earliest level of moral development resembles the amoral stage of Piaget (1932) in the sense that both of them imagined that morality and respect do not exist in the mind of infants or young children. However, Piaget did not explain much about this period except the domination of motor rules. Instead, Kohlberg (1969) analyzed this stage in detail, explaining that moral values are present more like concrete results and physical events such as prizes and chastisements. In this level, children tend to think that they are good and righteous as they receive rewards or bad and wrong as they get punishments.

Kohlberg's explanation of young children's behaviors in the preconventional level is similar to the description of the behavioristic approach to morality. Skinner (1971) viewed moral behaviors as conditioned reactions (i.e., obedience or disobedience) to the stimuli of the social environment (i.e., punishment or reward) like any other behaviors (see Ch. 1 for the further explanation of Skinner's ideas on morality). Like the idea of the behavioral approach, Kohlberg (1981, 2008) maintained that the behaviors of young children would be generally controlled by rewards and punishments, without a sharp distinction between moral and non-moral motives and actions, in the level of pre-conventional morality.

The level of conventional morality, which is found in children eight years of age and older, is composed of similar ideas to the stage of Piaget's heteronomy regarding the central aspects of children's attitudes toward the rules and authority of society. According to Kohlberg (2008), children at the level of conventional morality tend to believe that adults with authority can judge what is right or wrong and children should follow what adults decide. In the conventional morality level, the reference of judgments does not reside in the mind of the children; just as the heteronomy of Piaget, and the core of this morality consists in obedience to the rules and standards which authority figures teach and impose. Hence, children in this level are likely to think that that they may become moral by fulfilling the expectations of parents and other adults, upholding social norms, preserving the conventional order, and performing exemplary roles (Kohlberg, 1969).

The ideas of Kohlberg about the conventional level of morality resonate well with the understanding of Freud (1930) on morality, as young children search for approval from parents and try to conform to the self-ideals or typical moral images which they adopt in their relationships with parents (see Ch. 1 for the further explanation of Freud's ideas on morality). All these social and moral endeavors of children at this level are basically initiated by their perception of the power difference between children and adults (Freud, 1930) or the coercion of adults (Piaget, 1932). As they feel that they are not strong or mature enough to judge by themselves, children believe that they should succumb to or depend on the power or authority of adults. Unlike Freud, Kohlberg, however, did not view the conventional level as the only form of morality or the fully developed level of moral judgments but suggested that children should transcend this level to be genuine moral agents in a society.

The level of Kohlberg's post-conventional morality, which may appear in the reasoning of adolescents of about 13 years or older, corresponds to the stage of Piaget's autonomy in terms of internalized morality and mature reasoning capacity. Kohlberg (1969) envisioned that the source of moral values becomes internal and morality becomes differentiated from convention in the reasoning of the adolescents within this level. Just like the progress from heteronomy to autonomy in Piaget's theory, the reference of judgments transits from outside the individual to inside, in the developmental process from conventional to post-conventional morality. According to Kohlberg (1981, 2008), individuals in the post-conventional level understand both arbitrary and essential aspects of rules, partake in the construction of norms with shared internal senses of standards, rights, and duties (i.e., the contractual legalistic orientation stage), construe the significance and implication of an incident, without being attached only to the apparent features of the incident, and make judgments with moral principles which are logically valid and universally applicable (i.e., the principled orientation stage).

Do Children Differentiate Morality from Convention?

According to Kohlberg (2008), moral principles are the social ideals which become a foundation for the formulation of specific rules and regulations including prescriptive moral norms of behaviors. He explained them even as the principles of "conscience" (Kohlberg, 2008, p. 18). Individuals with the principles of conscience, which are ethical, logical, and universal, could make a decision to disobey the rules of government or traditional practices, if the rules or traditions contradict their moral ideals such as equality and justice. That is why Kohlberg (1981) mentioned Mahatma Gandhi and Martin Luther King as examples of post-conventional morality, suggesting that these morally mature individuals fully actualized their principles of conscience to stand against inhumane and immoral laws, conventions, and cultural practices. Like these examples, the reasoning of the individuals in the post-conventional level manifests the capacity to differentiate between morality and convention. Hence, it becomes clear in the stage theory of Kohlberg that true moral thinkers should go beyond a legal vision of morality, i.e., one's obedience to the existing rules and observance of customary practices. This way, Kohlberg explained thoroughly the importance of the distinction between morality and convention in moral development, just as Piaget underlined the importance of the transition from heteronomy to autonomy.

Divergence between Piaget and Kohlberg

Kohlberg's theory of moral development is based on Piaget's theory of both moral and cognitive development (Piaget, 1932, 1950; Piaget & Inhelder, 1969). As for the principal nature of developmental stages, Kohlberg (1969, 1981), like Piaget, suggested that an invariant order exists in the sequence of developmental stages of moral reasoning. As heteronomy must precede autonomy in the theory of Piaget, nobody can reach the post-conventional level without having passed through the conventional level according to Kohlberg. However, they suggested divergent ideas on the question of when children can distinguish between morality and convention. Piaget thought that this developmental achievement would take place at around eight years of age or older, whereas for Kohlberg, it was 13 years or older. It would be necessary to examine why Kohlberg thought only adolescents and adults could perform true moral reasoning to understand the implications of the divergence between them.

First, Kohlberg evaluated that the concepts of Piaget's autonomy and heteronomy do not fulfil the conditions of the concept of stage. There are at least three characteristics of stages; "structural whole" (i.e., stages are the constellations of related traits.), "invariant order" (i.e., the order of developmental stages is neither changeable nor irreversible.), and "hierarchical integration" (i.e., a higher stage integrates its lower stages with new elements and replaces them) (Kohlberg, 1981, pp. 136—137). The moral stages of Piaget fulfill the idea of structural whole, as each stage consists of a systematic integration of various components: Heteronomy consists of unilateral respect, constraint, coercive rules, etc., whereas autonomy is formed of mutual respect, cooperation, rational rules, etc. (Piaget, 1932). However, Piaget's theory fulfils only partially the concept of invariant order between heteronomy and autonomy, unlike the theory of Kohlberg. As Piaget (1932) suggested that autonomy cannot emerge without passing the stage of heteronomy, his ideas on the invariant order of stages in moral development remain in the sense of ontogenesis (i.e., the course of development of an individual organism), but not in the strict sense of irreversibility (i.e., once individuals reach an advanced stage, they do not return to previous stages). As it is common that adults with autonomy can make judgements based on heteronomy in an authoritarian environment, a sort of moral regression from autonomy to heteronomy can take place in the social reasoning of an individual from Piaget's point of view.

On the other hand, Piaget did not consider the possibility of hierarchical integration in the relationships between autonomy and heteronomy. Despite the advanced quality of autonomy, it neither replaces nor modifies totally the lower stage of morality, heteronomy.

In contrast to Piaget's theory of moral development, the hierarchical integration of stages becomes a developmental characteristic in the cognitive theory of Piaget as well as in the moral theory of Kohlberg. For Kohlberg, the coexistence of pre-conventional, conventional, and post-conventional morality is not possible due to the ideas of hierarchical integration, because individuals at the level of post-conventional morality do not rely on the patterns and methods of previous moral stages but reason and judge based on universal principles and resolve the conflicts to which the lower stages cannot find solutions. However, Piaget (1932) observed the simultaneous presence of the two forms of morality in an individual. Thus, he viewed autonomy and heteronomy not simply as two stages but also as the two forms of morality. As one form cannot integrate completely the other form, both forms can exist at the same time and can be applied selectively to relevant situations.

Secondly, Kohlberg thought that the stages of moral judgments should correspond to those of cognitive development. Although he suggested that moral development is not the mere result of cognitive development, Kohlberg (1981) argued that the stages of moral reasoning cannot emerge without the development of parallel cognitive stages (p. 138). The pre-conventional, conventional, and post-conventional levels of Kohlberg are parallel to the pre-operational, operational, and formal operational stages of Piaget. Kohlberg thought that the genuine morality of individuals appears only after the development of formal operational reasoning in the cognitive stages of Piaget (12 years of age or older, see Piaget, 1950; Piaget & Inhelder, 1969). That is why post-conventional reasoning can be found in at least 13-year-old adolescents. Owing to the relation between morality and cognition, the age of the most mature morality of Kohlberg's theory should be older than that of the mature cognition of Piaget's theory. Instead, Piaget did not integrate morality with cognition in terms of developmental stages. Historically, he did not publish his studies of the developmental stages of cognition when he presented his theories of moral development in 1932. Piaget still adhered to his classic theories of morality even after the completion of his stage theory of cognition. Thus, autonomy, the mature morality of Piaget's theory, can emerge in the reasoning of children of eight years of age or older who do not reach the highest stage of cognitive development. This way, Kohlberg and Piaget revealed differences in terms of their understanding of the relationship between cognitive and moral development and the ages of moral development.

It might be true that the moral theory of Kohlberg is more advanced than that of Piaget particularly in the level of theoretical consistency, as Kohlberg applied the ideas of stages to his theory in a complete manner and integrated the theory of cognitive development. However, the co-existence of the two forms of morality and the relatively early emergence of genuine moral reasoning in the theory of Piaget can be rather close to the social domain theory of Turiel, which was developed after the theory of Kohlberg. As reviewed previously, Turiel and his colleagues have found that three- or four-year-old children can distinguish between moral and conventional domain (see Smetana, 2006, 2013; Turiel, 1983, 2006). On the ground of the co-existence of moral and conventional reasoning and the early presence of the capacity to distinguish between these two types of reasoning, there can be no developmental sequence between the moral and conventional domains of social reasoning. Since these ideas of Turiel were scientifically proved and widely accepted (see Helwig, 1995; Helwig et al., 2013; Turiel, 1983, 2002; Smetana, 2006), the stage theory of Kohlberg has been seriously challenged in terms of theoretical frames and empirical findings.

A Transition from Stage to Domain

"There is an adult in every child and a child in every adult" (Piaget, 1932, p. 85). This enigmatic phrase conveys indirectly the idea of the co-existence of different types of judgments in an individual. Basically, Piaget viewed autonomy as the morality of adults and heteronomy as that of children. With that phrase, however, he suggested that children with a capacity for cooperation can reason like adults and adults sometimes cannot judge in a mature manner. In other words, children can become autonomous moral agents like adults through their experience of cooperation with peers as equals with an attitude of mutual respect. Instead, adults can remain as heteronomous thinkers in a certain condition by simply following what others ask them to do despite their autonomy. The idea of Piaget that both types of morality can be found in older children as well as adults resonates well with Turiel's theory, which is based on the presence of diverse domains in reasoning.

The idea of the simultaneous existence and development of conventional and moral domains contradicts the stage theories of moral development and results in a transition from stage to domain in terms of the basic unit of developmental analysis. For Kohlberg (1969, 1971), individuals with mature morals (i.e., post-conventional morality) do not need to maintain the conventional reasoning of lower stages (i.e., conventional morality). According to the domain approach, conventional reasoning cannot be replaced by moral reasoning or vice versa, as these two domains of reasoning exist as independent systems of knowledge with different characteristics from early childhood. Turiel (1983, 2006) envisioned that two independent trajectories of development would exist in the moral and conventional domains of social reasoning, respectively. Therefore, it is necessary to examine in what domain(s) the reasoning of children takes place and what kind of developmental path is formulated in a domain in the studies of children's social reasoning.

In social life, quite a few issues and happenings tend to be complex and the reasoning of individuals about them is not always subjected to a clear-cut distinction between moral and conventional domains. To discern the difference between the two, it is useful to apply the concepts of intrinsic and extrinsic values. A moral decision or action is valuable for its own sake (i.e., intrinsic value), whereas a convention is valuable for the sake of something else (i.e., extrinsic value) (see Zimmerman & Bradley, 2019). This classification of domains by the nature of value is plausible in many situations, especially when the relationship between the two is understood. For example, driving a car on the righthand side of the road as a convention does not have any greater internal worth in itself than driving it on the left. Nevertheless, the violation of this rule influences some intrinsic values such as the wellbeing of people. In this case, the observance of the rule has moral implications, although the rule is not valuable for its own sake. Thus, it is significant to view the nature of a rule or practice and its connection to other values. In addition, it is important to distinguish between moral and legal obligation. Some behaviors such as physical violence and theft are bounded legally as well as morally. However, many moral operations are independent of legal obligations. For instance, some people feed the homeless. They do it due to the intrinsic worth of this charitable service, even though no law obliges them to do it. Fundamentally, what makes one's actions morally honorable is not their obedience to the law, which is extrinsic to them, but the intrinsic values of their intentions and operations. Thus, discerning the intrinsic values of judgments facilitates a distinction between moral and conventional thinking and an in-depth analysis of social reasoning.

It is challenging to identify and classify the domains involved in complex incidents. However, it is also very true that most incidents in daily life are not as complicated as the Heinz dilemma that Kohlberg (1969, 1981, see footnote 1 in this chapter) adopted for his empirical studies. Moreover, the complexity of life should not blur the distinction between morality and convention but encourage researchers to examine how various domains of social reasoning interact in the reasoning of individuals. If one ignores the distinction between the two and the interaction between them, it is easy to get lost in the analyses of the multifaceted phenomenon of many events in society. Instead, the distinction between morality and convention based on the presence or absence of the intrinsic worth of actions leads researchers to analyze substantially how children and adults participate in the constitution of judgments and the establishment of norms in order to promote justice and harmony in their social life. Furthermore, it is always important to remember that individuals with power and authority can devalue and disregard the human rights of weak and poor people in the name of law and tradition. From the people's point of view, the oppressed and exploited humans can liberate themselves from the burdens of unjust conventions and regulations only when they understand and declare the absence of the intrinsic worth of oppressive practices, denounce the presence of the inhumane aspects of the practice, and enter into a democratic procedure to construct new standards based on social justice and human rights.

5

Does Freedom Help Children Become Moral?

In 1964, students at the University of California, Berkeley initiated the Free Speech Movement. In those days in the United States of America, the political activities of students on the campus were not permitted. Several students stood up to realize their right to freedom of speech. This movement inspired many other students in numerous universities and became a starting point of a student movement for civil rights. (See Free Speech Movement | UC Berkeley Library, n.d.)

Young people who engaged in the Free Speech Movement made a decision to disobey the laws of the government which constrained their freedom of expression and assembly in the university. According to the moral stage theory of Kohlberg (1970, 1981), this type of civil disobedience can be an example of the post-conventional level of moral judgments. The students made a judgment to stand against the laws that banned freedom of speech and to live beyond the unjust conventional constraints of the government according to universal moral values. As they knew that the laws of a democratic nation should not violate basic human rights, they could not simply obey in silence to what the authorities demanded but exercised their freedom to protest against the unjust regulations of government.

I am curious how the university students of the Free Speech Movement learned to develop their personal freedom in adolescence and how their commitment to human rights was connected with their freedom of choice in childhood. It would not be easy to find specific answers to this question, but it is possible to examine how the rudimentary exercise of freedom in the early period of development influences the formation of moral values. Nucci (1981), one of the pioneering scholars of social domain theory, suggested that children's freedom of choice in personal matters helps their moral development. In this chapter, I would like to review his studies and create a theoretical frame for the analysis of freedom in the domains of social reasoning.

First, I will evaluate whether the freedom of children on personal issues is related to moral development according to social domain theory. Nucci (1981; Nucci & Turiel, 1978) constructed the concept of the personal domain, which consists of judgments according to personal likes and dislikes, and examined how the development of this domain would contribute to the progress of moral development. Secondly, I will review the interaction between personal and non-personal domains, i.e., conventional and moral. I will examine how some issues in the conventional domain become part of the personal domain as children grow and how the development of moral judgments interacts with the various features of the personal domain. Thirdly, I will discuss the relationship between freedom and discipline in children's social development. Although freedom and discipline seem to be discordant, children should develop their freedom while regulating their emotions and actions according to social norms and moral values in order to become competent members of society. Lastly, I will adopt the theory of Sen (1985, 2006) on the types of freedom, i.e., well-being freedom and agency freedom in order to discuss how the two types of freedom are present in the domains of social reasoning and suggest a need to study the interaction between reasoning and freedom from a developmental perspective.

Freedom of Choice and Moral Development

According to Nucci (1983, 1996), children's practices of free choices contribute to the development of children's reasoning on autonomy, agency, privacy, and moral judgments. As children make simple judgments in daily life on what to eat, wear, and play according to their likes and dislikes, they grow in self-knowledge and become active agents in their relationships with adults and peers. Furthermore, children construct a rudimentary idea of human rights as they understand the boundary of personal decisions and develop eventually a sense of privacy. As the conception of human rights is an essential part of moral reasoning, it can be construed that the practice of personal choice influences the moral development of children. From the social domain approach, the effect of freedom of choice on moral development has been a main theme of the studies on the relationship between the personal and moral domains (see Nucci et al., 2013).

Before the examination of the association between the personal and moral domains, it may be beneficial to think about two contrary views on the relationship between freedom and morality in order to have a broad view on this issue. Some people tend to view freedom and morality as oppositional, whereas others, as interdependent. In other words, some believe that the exercises of freedom result in immoral behaviors and the moral norms of society constrain the freedom of individuals. By contrast, others suggest that freedom is an essential part of moral reasoning and the moral judgments and actions of individuals contribute to the enhancement of their freedom. This divergence can originate from their different views on morality. When some believe that morality lies in their conformity to the established rules of society, they are likely to maintain that individuals become moral by restricting personal freedom. Instead, when people believe that morality consists of the realization of their capacities to think freely, based on social ideals, and formulate rules and laws to enhance human dignities, they are likely to maintain that freedom is an essential component of morality and an indispensable condition for a just society. The latter view on a positive relationship between morals and freedom resonates well with the understanding of morality from a cognitive developmental perspective. The autonomous morality of Piaget (1932), the post-conventional morality of Kohlberg (1969), and the moral domain of Turiel (1983) emphasize the capacities of individuals to think, speak, and act freely according to their own moral ideals such as social justice and human rights. From this perspective, it is appropriate to regard the freedom of children as the foundation of moral reasoning.

From the social domain approach, the interdependence of freedom and morality is reviewed initially in the studies on the influence of the personal domain on the development of moral reasoning (Nucci, 1996; Nucci et al., 2013). Children can identify a certain sphere of events, practices and activities in which they can exercise their freedom of choice according not to the norms given by adults or moral principles, but to their preferences. This discovery of children's capacity to judge by their own standards meaningfully enriches the comprehension of children's social reasoning. However, freedom of choice does not include specific ethical norms or social ideals. It is not part of morality, but of the personal domain. Acknowledging the difference between the two, I will review how the concept of the personal domain has developed and how this domain interacts with the moral and conventional domains.

The Presence of the Personal Domain of Social Reasoning

Nucci (1981, 1996, 2013) confirmed the presence of the personal domain in the social reasoning of children and observed developmental changes in the personal through empirical studies. According to Nucci (1996), "The personal refers to the set of actions that the individual considers to be outside of the area of justifiable social regulation. These actions are subject not to considerations of right and wrong, but to preferences and choice" (p. 42). The personal is one of the domains of social reasoning, i.e., the coherent systems of thinking which children construct by participating in social interactions and classifying varying characteristics of social events. As reviewed in the previous chapter, Turiel and his colleagues (Turiel, 1978, 1983; Nucci & Turiel, 1978; Smetana, 1981b) identified moral and conventional judgments as two distinctive domains of social reasoning. Along with these two, the personal domain was added as an independent system in the social reasoning of children.

Nucci (1981) asked students from the second grade of elementary school up to university in the United States if the action presented was wrong even in the absence of standards. He presented typical actions in three domains; moral, conventional, and personal. The examples of the moral domain were theft and hitting; the conventional, chewing gum in the classroom and calling a professor by name; and the personal, holding the content of one's correspondence private and keeping his hair long as a boy. According to the research, almost all participants estimated that all the transgressions of the moral domain were wrong regardless of the presence or absence of social norms. Instead, the actions of the conventional domain would have been considered wrong if there were the corresponding rules. For example, if there is a rule "do not eat in class," they would judge it wrong to take food during the lesson. Without the rule, they can judge it differently. In the end, the actions of the personal domain tended to be considered outside of the normative regulations, but subjected to one's own decisions. For example, the children and adolescents of this research thought that the length of hair and the choice of friend should be a "person's business" (Nucci, 1981, p. 120). It was, thus, suggested that three distinct domains, i.e., personal, conventional, and moral are present in the social reasoning of children and adolescents.

In addition, Nucci (1981) examined the seriousness of possible transgressions regarding moral, conventional, and personal events. He found that students at all ages saw that conflicts in the personal domain were the least serious problems. For example, they tended to see "interacting with a friend forbidden by parents" as a personal matter and believed that this type of action was not as problematic as conventional or moral transgressions. From the perspective of children and adolescents, the weight and implication of conflicts and transgressions regarding personal matters were significantly different from those in the moral and conventional domains. Based on the observation of these variations, thus, it was confirmed that the personal domain exists as an independent system of social reasoning, along with the moral and conventional domains (see Nucci, 2013 Nucci, Camino, & Sapiro, 1996; Nucci & Smetana, 1996; Smetana, 2006; Turiel, 2006a).

The Nature of the Personal Domain

The discovery of the personal domain signifies that children understand their capacity to know, express, and exercise their freedom to make a choice regarding various issues without asking permission from parents, considering the regulations of community, worrying about any negative consequences on the welfare of others, or reflecting on social ideals such as respect and justice. In other words, the personal domain of social reasoning is mainly made up of thoughts concerning individuals' preferences and choices in the realm of their private life (Nucci, 1981, 1996; Perkins & Turiel, 2007). Therefore, conventional practices, social norms, and universal moral principles are not supposed to directly regulate the specific judgments of children and adults in the personal.

The personal domain possesses a particular justification and formal feature of reasoning, which differentiates it from the conventional and moral domains. First, a main justification for judgments over the relevant issues of the personal domain consists in personal preferences. Children and adolescents explain why they make a certain judgment in the personal by simply saying "I like it." They do not need to justify their judgments about their preferences over food and dress with social norms or moral ideals. For instance, the choice of a girl over what film to watch alone on the weekend does not influence any public order or group functions. However, it is different when a group of girls with varying interests tries to decide what film to watch. This process of finding a consensus or arriving at an agreement in a group is part of conventional judgments.

Secondly, the formal criterion of judgments in the personal domain is to be epitomized as freedom of choice. A judgment in the personal domain does not depend on the norms of society or on universal moral principles, but is actualized by the exercise of personal freedom to choose what one likes. In terms of relations with social norms, it can be first said that both personal and moral domains are not fundamentally constrained by the existing laws of society. In Piagetian terms, both personal and moral judgments are not heteronomous but autonomous, as they are not dependent on explicit rules outside individuals but on the inner criteria of decision-makers. Although judgments in the personal sphere do not possess all the components of autonomous morality in Piaget's theory, such as mutual respect and cooperation, they represent the independent capacities of children to understand their uniqueness and choose freely according to their self-knowledge rather than the indications of others or of institutions. Then, the choices of children in this domain are not about "ought to" but "want" as there are no normative aspects in specific judgments, unlike in the conventional and moral domains. If a boy wants a blue cap, he puts it on his head for an outing. However, if he attends a special event at school and should respect a dress code for that occasion, he ought to follow it. This judgment belongs to the conventional domain, as his choice of clothes is not regulated by his freedom but by the authority or norms of his school. In this manner, freedom of choice becomes a formal characteristic for differentiation between personal and non-personal domains.

Moreover, it should be noted that the judgments belonging to the personal domain do not have any special intrinsic or universal values in them, unlike moral judgments, but the presence of this domain is valuable for its own sake across cultures. For example, a girl prefers the subway to a bus when she visits her relatives. When both means are equally efficient, there is no way to judge that the subway is more valuable than the bus. In many cases, a specific personal choice like this may not possess any significant universal worth. However, it does not imply that the presence of the personal domain is not intrinsically valuable. This domain is closely connected to the rights of children to share freely what they feel and think and express their ideas on the issues that affect their welfare (see *The Convention on the Rights of the Child*, n.d.). The personal choices of children should be universally respected and guaranteed as long as they do not infringe others' rights or damage their own well-being.

Thus, I suggest that the presence of the personal domain and the practice of free choice in this domain are closely connected to the intrinsic and universal values of the freedom and rights of children.

Although there are some typical issues of the personal such as hobby and menu selection, it is difficult to specify what types of judgments or issues belong to the personal domain due to variations by culture, gender, and age. For instance, people in some cultural groups believe that women are not supposed to wear trousers or jeans. This belief is part of the conventional reasoning in these cultures unlike the many others in which people consider it to be a personal choice. Even in the same cultural environment, there can be individual variations in the understanding of the personal. For an example from a school, students may view the length of hair as their own business, whereas teachers want to create a rule on the length of hair for the pupils. This contrast implies that the students view implicitly this issue as a part of the personal unlike the teachers who regard it as a convention. Because of differences in the same cultural group regarding the understanding of the domain of an issue, arguments over the transgressions of conventional norms can take place. Although there should be no regulations on issues in the personal domain, parents and teachers may exercise constraints over the issues which children believe to be their own business.

The Personal Domain and the Interactions between Mother and Child

Nucci and Weber (1995) observed the interactions between mother and child in middle-class families in the U.S. and interviewed them in order to examine how young children develop their conceptions of the personal domain and differentiate them from the moral and conventional domains. According to the results of their studies, the mothers revealed a distinction between the personal and the other domains in terms of their permitting freedom to their children. They were more likely to allow children to make a choice according to their preferences regarding the activities pertinent to the personal domain such as clothing, play, the type and amount of food, friends, etc. On the other hand, they did not allow their children such freedom in the issues related to their children's welfare and convention. According to Nucci et al. (2013), children are likely to comply with the instructions of their mother about conventional and moral issues (e.g., how to behave at table, not taking the toy of another child) without showing resistance. However, even four- or five-year-old children do not want to obey the maternal directives which constrain their freedom over personal issues. In short, young children understand that they have freedom to choose or authority to decide regarding personal issues, but admit the authority of adults over moral or conventional actions.

Nucci et al. (1996) found the same results regarding the presence of the personal in mother-child interactions in Brazil. There were, however, age differences in the emergence of the distinction between the personal and the non-personal according to social class in Brazil. The children of lower-class families tended to identify the personal issues later than those of the middle-class. This finding indicates that it is a misunderstanding to view that this developmental phenomenon is to be found only in Western or individualistic cultures (Nucci, 1996). Even though it is true that the use of terms such as freedom of choice or personal preference is rather common in certain cultures, the presence of the personal in social reasoning along with moral and conventional domains has been confirmed across cultures.

Nucci and his colleagues (Nucci, 1996; Nucci & Weber, 1995, Nucci & Smetana, 1996; Nucci et al., 1996) reflected on why mothers invite children to exercise their freedom of choice. Particularly, Nucci and Smetana (1996) suggested that American mothers of young children think that the children's experience of making a choice over certain things is conducive to the development of competency, autonomy, and agency (p. 47). The free choices of children allow them to develop children's mastery and power to control, foster the development of a positive sense of self and self-esteem, and help them to grow in a sense of being an autonomous individual. The belief of mothers about the importance of personal choice for child development implies that the children's exercise of freedom of choice is not an option but an essential aspect of child-rearing. In other words, mothers should give the children freedom of choice in order for them to become active, capable, and independent individuals in a society. However, mothers agree that compromise regarding the boundary of children's freedom is an inevitable aspect of the child-mother interactions. While mothers acknowledge a need to indicate the limits of children's free choices, they are willing to negotiate with children over them (Nucci & Weber, 1995; Nucci & Smetana, 1996). This sort of negotiation can become rather common as children grow and reach their adolescence. In sum, mothers understand the importance of freedom of choice as well as the necessity of interactions with children about this issue for the growth of their children.

When children cannot express their own preferences and opinions over personal issues such as what games they like to play and who they want to play with, children may have difficulties in their development and suffer from some psychological disorders (see Nucci, 1996, Nucci et al., 2013). Hasebe et al. (2004) found that adolescents in both Japan and the United States are more likely to reveal psychopathological problems such as depression, anxiety, and somatization when they perceive the control of parents over their behaviors in the personal domain. By contrast, parental control over issues about conventional rules and practices was not associated with psychological problems. In addition, no gender differences were found in the U.S., whereas these symptoms were found to be more pervasive among girls than boys regardless of age in Japan. This cultural difference indicates that Japanese female adolescents tend to be controlled by parents over the issues of the personal domain more than male peers and to be educated to be submissive to the authority of adults (Hasebe et al., 2004, p. 825). Personal freedom is crucial for a healthy human growth regardless of gender and culture. Children should be allowed to create the boundary of privacy and personal control and develop autonomy (see Turiel, 2002).

The Influence of the Personal Domain on Moral Development

Erikson (1977) emphasized the importance of free choice for the development of young children. He maintained that parents should teach their children well to experience the autonomy of free choice in a gradual manner, so that children can develop a conscience in an appropriate period and explore their environment widely. As Erikson indicated the steady nature of the development of children's autonomy, most mothers and children tend to expand progressively the boundary of children's free choice. Nucci and Weber (1995) studied the expanding process of children's freedom in their relationship with mothers and found that mothers initially introduce boundaries to children and children may or may not accept them. When they do not agree with mothers, children can initiate negotiations with them over the boundaries of personal issues. In some cases, they may vigorously resist the suggestions of parents and strongly claim their freedom over certain issues. This sort of negotiation and resistance regarding personal freedom helps children to formulate the concept of human rights (Nucci, 1996, p. 46).

Nucci (1996; Nucci et al., 2013) reflected on the influence of the development of the personal domain on the emergence of moral conceptions along two paths; the comprehension of unique personalities, and the understanding of others as independent agents. First, children develop their self-knowledge in the evolving process of the conception of the personal domain, and, in turn, their understanding of the self assists them to construct the idea of their own rights. In this process, self-knowledge and personal freedom interact reciprocally for the formation of the rudimentary idea of human rights. On the one hand, the understanding of the self enables children to exercise personal freedom. Children recognize their unique tastes and styles and know that they themselves have to express them to engage in interpersonal relationships as independent agents. On the other hand, the practice of personal freedom enables children to appreciate their own uniqueness. The personal preferences are not always certain. They can change and need to be confirmed. As children make free choices over familiar and unfamiliar things, they can evaluate the results of the choices and upgrade their understanding about their tastes and styles. In the process of mutual reinforcement between self-knowledge and personal freedom, children develop the ideas of the personal domain and acknowledge the ownership of the knowledge of the self which others cannot replace. Thus, children's recognition of their personal capacity for freedom and of the irreplaceability of self-knowledge becomes an essential part of the conceptualization of human rights.

Secondly, Nucci (1996) assumed that children can view others as independent agents with their own thoughts and feelings since they begin to construct the sense of agency through the conceptualization of the personal domain (p. 57). At an early age, children understand the differences between their interactions with other persons and those with objects such as toys. Through this distinction, they come to grasp the unique patterns of interactions with others who have their own thoughts and emotions, and deepen their knowledge about their own needs, desires, and capacities. As children understand themselves as agents with their own boundaries of personal choices and capacities for freedom, they come to know that other individuals also have their unique ideas and tendencies. When children understand both others and themselves as agents, they are able to enter into the formative process of mutual respect and cooperation.

Nucci (1996) adopted the idea of Piaget (1932) to suggest that the influence of the personal on moral development is mediated by mutual respect and cooperation. The emergence of the personal domain helps children to conceptualize the mutual respect and cooperation which develop autonomous morality. However, it is important not to presuppose that the relationship between the personal and the moral is causal or unidirectional. It is also plausible that the development of the moral domain influences that of the personal domain. Especially when children view themselves and others as independent agents, they can develop a sense of fairness and compare their boundaries of personal issues to those of other peers. For instance, when children observe that their friends have more things to choose personally than they have, they can enter into a dialogue with or initiate an argument against parents based on their judgments about needs for great freedom or fair treatment. In sum, the emergence of the personal is closely connected to the knowledge of others, which facilitates the development of mutuality and cooperation and the reciprocal interaction between the personal and moral domains of social reasoning.

Relationship between Personal and Non-personal Domains

Turiel and Nucci (Turiel, 1983, 2002, 2006, 2013; Nucci, 1983, 1991, 1996; Nucci et al, 2013) found that differentiations between personal, conventional and moral domains take place in early childhood and these domains develop independently and interdependently through childhood and adolescence. Thus, it is important to note that the personal domain does not evolve by itself in isolation, but in conjunction with other domains of social reasoning. Especially, the developmental features of the personal are closely connected to other principal issues in child development such as autonomy, self, parent-child interactions, the psychological well-being of the child, etc. For a wide comprehension of child development, I would like to discuss how personal and non-personal domains in social reasoning are interconnected and how the personal freedom of children is expressed and actualized in different domains.

The Personal and the Conventional

The fluidity of the personal boundaries by gender, age, and culture implies that of the conventional boundaries as well. In general, the judgments of authority figures in the conventional domain can delineate the range of the personal especially for the liberty of young children. For example, a family has a rule to have dinner together at 7 PM and allows children to play outside before the dinner. In this conventional context, they may exercise personal freedom of choice in a limited manner. They can decide to come home from the playground at 5 PM or just a couple of minutes before 7 PM according to their desires. While the boundary of the personal domain tends to be regulated by the conventional domain, it is likely to expand in the course of child development. In this expansion, the exercises of personal choices influence the conventional practices of family or community. Returning to the example of the dinner time of a family, parents have to rethink the practice to dine together every evening as children grow older and prefer to stay late with friends outside. Although this process of change may cause conflicts between parents and children, the family should accept a need to modify and reformulate the traditions and rules for the growth of children and the preservation of family ties in an ever-evolving social milieu.

When the domain attribution of an issue is not understood in the same manner by parents and children, the methods of judgments differ between them. For example, some mothers may believe that they have to make a choice over afterschool activities for their children (i.e., conventional), whereas children claim that they should decide what to do (i.e., personal). Some fathers give their children specific indications regarding legitimate places for play and ask children to obey them (i.e., conventional), whereas children believe that they can freely choose the places where they play with friends (i.e., personal). These variations between parents and children are causes of conflicts in the family. In terms of the methods of decision-making, conventional issues need the order of authority or the consensus of members in a group, whereas personal issues do not require the consent or permission of another person, but only the free choices of agents. When children and parents think differently about the question of who can make a decision, they have no choice but to face conflicts in their interactions. It is important, however, to consider that these conflicts help them to realize a need for dialogue and negotiation. Parents and children may discuss related issues to understand one another and seek agreement.

The importance of dialogue and discussion between children and adults is manifest for the development of children in general (see Hoffman, 2000). The children's practice of free choice within the rigid boundary fixed by parents does not help them sufficiently to develop a sense of agency and autonomy. Instead, the practice of free choice needs to be coupled with the parent-child interactions which adjust the boundary of the personal liberty of children. The quality of the parent-child interactions is certainly related to parenting styles. Thus, it is worthwhile to compare two parenting styles, i.e., authoritative and authoritarian, in order to review the importance of dialogue between parents and children.

According to Baumrind (1966, 1989, 1991, 2005), authoritative parents usually direct their children's activities in a rational and consistent manner. While they set rules and standards in a clear manner for their children, regulate them in a firm and constant manner, and control their divergent behaviors, they encourage their children to be independent and understand their rights and limits. In contrast, authoritarian parents are strict disciplinarians and generate the standards of conduct. In accordance with the standards, they attempt to form, regulate, and evaluate the behaviors and attitudes of their children. They tend to value obedience as a virtue and punish their children in order to correct disobedient behavior. They do not communicate with their children in a reciprocal manner as equals but ask them to accept whatever they instruct. The crucial difference between the two parenting styles lies in the quality of communication. Unlike authoritarian parents, authoritative ones promote interactive conversations with their children and talk about the reasons behind their policies and standards. Empirical studies support that authoritative parenting is positively associated with socially acceptable and morally sound behaviors in children (see Baumrind et al., 2010).

In an open and effective communication with parents, children can practice thinking independently, express what they think, learn to listen to others, and arrive at an agreement. In the developmental process of the personal domain, what used to be under the dynamics of the conventional (i.e., the authority of adults) can become a matter of children's freedom. Certainly, some rules which used to be effective for the upbringing of children are no longer necessary for them. However, personal freedom cannot be allowed to children without limit and the boundary between children and parents needs to be clearly maintained for healthy family dynamics (see Nichols & Schwartz, 2001). When this process of personal growth takes place through parent-child dialogue with mutual respect, children can become free, autonomous, and collaborative with respect to personal as well as conventional matters.

Integration between the Personal and Moral Domains of Social Reasoning

Nucci (1996) applied the concept of autonomy to integrate the personal and moral domains. According to Piaget (1932), autonomy represents the type of morality which belongs to older children and adults. When children believe that they can modify the rules of games by mutual agreement among them, it is assumed that they have arrived at the level of autonomous morality. As this concept does not focus on the free choices of children, but on the comprehension and modification of rules, it does not perfectly correspond to the autonomy of the personal domain based on personal likes and dislikes. Despite the difference between the two types of autonomy, they can appear at the same time in the parent-child negotiations over the guidelines of family life. When children are not willing to obey some rules of the family, they may enter into conversations with parents so as to modify them or formulate new ones. In this case, they could achieve both aspects of autonomy, which are the free choice of activity (i.e., the formal feature of the personal) as well as the capacity to modify the existing rules (i.e., a main aspect of autonomous morality). Thus, it may be assumed that children develop their autonomy by exercising freedom of choice in the personal domain and participating in negotiations with parents over the boundary of their personal authority. In turn, the development of autonomy in the personal domain helps them exercise their authority and ability as autonomous individuals to constitute new rules and modify old ones for their civil society together with others in the spirit of mutual respect and cooperation.

Erikson (1977) suggested, "The sense of autonomy fostered in the child and modified as life progresses, serves (and is served by) the preservation in economic and political life of a sense of justice" (p. 229). He mainly conceptualized the idea of autonomy in a general manner as being free from the intervention of others or rejecting the control of others. For Erikson, autonomy itself is not a type of morality, like for Piaget, but is considered as a seed of moral reasoning. This idea resembles the observation of Nucci (1996) that children endeavor to establish a zone of free choice, in which they can exercise their own authority as an independent person. In the conceptualization process of the personal domain, children develop their knowledge of their uniqueness and identity and become autonomous and cooperative individuals with a capacity for moral reasoning. In this context, the relationship between the development of the personal and moral domains reveals a close interconnectedness. According to Nucci (1996), children may not grow in a healthy and balanced manner when either personal or moral reasoning is missing. The exercise of free choice without a sense of morality such as fairness can result in egoistic behaviors, whereas the application of moral principles without a respect for personal issues can damage seriously the psychological well-being of children. Only when the personal and the moral develop hand in hand, children can grow as autonomous individuals with moral consciousness.

Discipline and Freedom

The development of autonomy as a seed of morality is closely connected to the quality of interaction between parents and children. When parents adopt an appropriate discipline method, they can help their children to grow autonomously and morally (Grusec et al., 2013; Hoffman, 1970, 2000; Hoffman & Saltzstein, 1967; Kuczynski & Knafo, 2013; see Nieman & Shea, 2004). The common methods of parental discipline that researchers have found are induction (reasoning or inductive reasoning), love withdrawal, and power assertion. First, induction signifies that parents explain to children appropriate reasons for good behaviors and negative consequences of misconducts. Then, love withdrawal indicates that adults refuse to speak or listen to children, stop expressing their affection to them, and express their disappointment. Lastly, power assertion usually indicates the punishments of adults such as spanking or verbal threats. Among these disciplines, only induction results in positive changes in the behaviors of children across cultures (Hoffman, 1970, 2000).

The effectiveness of induction in moral development has been confirmed by the cognitive approach (Kohlberg, 1969; Piaget, 1932; Smetana, 1999; Turiel, 2006a) as well as the socialization approach (see Grusec el al., 2013). For parents, it is important to understand that induction differs from any types of verbal punishment which elicit shame and a sort of anxiety or fear. According to Helwig et al. (2013), children negatively evaluate parental acts of disciplines based on shaming and believed that these acts damage their feelings of psychological well-being and self-worth. Across cultures, children can learn to be autonomous and moral by participating in negotiations with parents in order to agree on a boundary for their personal freedom and by attending to the disciplinary encounters with parents which value their rationality and responsibility (see Kochanska et al., 2003).

In the personal domain, most agree that children's freedom of choice needs to be regulated by and negotiated with parents. As this freedom in the personal domain is related to a particular thing or activity, it makes sense to acknowledge its limit in real life. Simply, no persons can possess and do all that they want. However, as an abstract concept, freedom contradicts a limit or boundary and transcends it. As it is related to the ideals and capacities which individuals want to achieve without restriction, it should be open to new possibilities. However, from a developmental perspective, this openness of freedom does not imply that children and adults do not need any discipline or can pursue just whatever they desire to realize their ideals. Although freedom and discipline seem to be incompatible, young individuals should develop their freedom while governing their activities according to diverse social and moral values and pursuing a harmony with others in the community. Since freedom means neither the absence of order nor the manifestation of egoism, certain types of freedom can be disciplined and restricted in order to protect the welfare of people and promote fairness (see Helwig, 1998; Turiel & Wainryb, 1998).

Most governments endorse civil liberties such as freedom of expression and of religion but restrict them in some cases. In South Korea, the parliament passed a law which bans sending balloons which contain anti-North Korea leaflets (Kuhn, 2020). Some activists in South Korea floated big balloons to spread the leaflets and other types of materials which criticized and condemned the North Korean government and policies. Their activities provoked North Korea and increased the military tensions on the border between the North and the South, near which many civilians live and work. The government of South Korea decided to restrict the freedom of those activists to send those materials to the North. Although some criticized this law, the majority of members of congress and people were supportive of the legislation of this ban for the security of the country and agreed to restrict the freedom of some civilians. Likewise, the exercise of freedom should be accompanied by reasoning about the specific conditions and consequences of free actions. In this way, freedom and discipline can work together to promote welfare and security based on the reasoning of people (see Snyder, 2016).

From a developmental perspective, Helwig (1995) conducted a study with adolescents and young adults in the U.S. to examine how they make judgments when freedom of speech creates a conflict with other concerns such as legal norms, physical harm, psychological damage, and equality. When this freedom was presented as being in conflict with the law, most participants affirmed the freedom of speech. They explained why freedom of speech should be guaranteed in various ways. For instance, freedom of speech helps people pursue truth, makes society progress, and holds moral and political ideals upright. This result indicates that adolescents understand the concept of civil liberty and make a judgment according not to the extrinsic norms but the intrinsic moral values. However, their judgments were different when the conflict between the freedom and other concerns was salient. For example, the conflict between the freedom of speech and psychosocial harm was presented to the participants with a hypothetical situation in which an individual addresses a speech in a public place including disrespectful expressions toward an ethnic minority group. In this situation, the participants often subordinated the freedom of speech to other moral concerns. This freedom surely is part of human rights. Nevertheless, when one's rights are not compatible with others' welfare, some may endorse the restriction of the rights. Just as freedom of choice in the personal domain has a limiting boundary, freedom of speech in the moral domain can be circumscribed due to other conflicting moral concerns. This limitation implies that children and adolescents consider not only freedom but also other social and moral concerns and integrate them in their judgments.

The finding that adolescents often subordinate freedom to other concerns may imply that the disciplinary intervention of parents and teachers works for them when it is logically consistent and morally acceptable. A genuine discipline aims to make children and adolescents cherish the value of freedom and help them exercise it in a rational manner. For instance, when parents and children enter into a communal reasoning process in the spirit of mutual respect, like the method of induction, to construct the boundary of the personal choice of children, children can experience various freedoms such as freedom of choice, expression, and participation, which touch all the main domains of social reasoning. Instead, lack of this type of discipline encounter in a family retards and hinders the social development of children. With a belief that freedom and discipline can go hand in hand, it would be important to devise the disciplinary methods which enhance the freedom of children and adolescents.

Freedom and Domain

I have reviewed the studies of Nucci (1981; Nucci & Weber, 1995) and Helwig (1995) on freedom of choice and freedom of expression. As I raised a question of whether the freedom of choice in the personal domain is related to the freedom of speech in the moral domain, it is necessary to examine their studies based on social domain theory. It might not be difficult to hypothesize that the two types of freedom are closely connected and to presuppose that freedom of choice helps children develop the conceptions of human rights and civil liberties. However, no specific empirical studies seem to have been done to answer this question from the domain approach. For the improvement of research on freedom, I believe that the relationship between freedom and domain needs to be conceptualized substantially with a refined comprehension of freedom. Thus, it is necessary to question how to construct diverse conceptions of freedom and study the relationship between them in light of the domain distinction. As this question has not been thoroughly examined by the researchers of social domain theory, I would like to examine the ideas of Sen (1985, 2006) on freedom and discuss them from the domain perspective.

Amartya Sen, the winner of the Nobel Prize in economics in 1998, examined the issues of freedom in the context of human development. Sen (1985, 2006) distinguished two types of freedom, which are well-being freedom and agency freedom. The former refers to the various capabilities of individuals which are necessary to secure and enhance the corresponding aspects of their well-being, whereas the latter signifies the intentions and actions of individuals to realize the ideals and objectives which are valuable for them as well as for others (Sen, 2006, p. 91). Certainly, these two types of freedom are essential for the social and moral development of children. And it is possible to think about applying these types of freedom to the distinctive domains of social reasoning.

Well-being freedom can be specified in all the domains of social reasoning. Basically, any individual and collective choices of a specific object, activity, and policy for the enhancement of human wellness can be part of this freedom. In the personal domain, the well-being freedom of Sen (2006) is certainly compatible with the free choices of children, which realize their likes and avoid their dislikes and help them grow as automounts individuals. In the moral domain, freedom of conscience, freedom of worship, and freedom of association can be good examples of well-being freedom. One of the principal justifications for moral judgments revolves around concerns for the protection and development of human welfare (Turiel, 1983; Smetana, 2006). In terms of empirical studies, Nucci (1981; Nucci & Weber, 1995) examined freedom of choice (i.e., personal domain) and Helwig (1995) dealt with freedom of expression (i.e., moral domain). According to their studies, both children and adults understand that their freedoms in the personal and moral domains contribute to the development of their capabilities and the enhancement of their welfare and rights. Thus, applications of Sen's concept of well-being freedom to the personal and moral domains can confirm the results of the previous studies according to the social domain approach and enrich their implications.

Regarding the conventional domain of social reasoning, however, no empirical study seems to have been conducted to examine the issue of freedom with respect to social conventions and cultural practices. Because this domain is closely associated with judgments based on established norms, conventional reasoning seems to be distant from free choice or free decision. Nevertheless, it is a mistake to equate this domain with obedience to the existing rules of communities. In contrast, it is crucial to acknowledge that the conventional reasoning of individuals includes the establishment and modification of social rules and regulations, which are the collective activities of free social agents for the well-being of people. The exercise of freedom in the conventional domain can be also found in the activities of children. The study of Piaget (1932) on the game rules of children is relevant to well-being freedom in the conventional domain. Children about eight years of age or older can change the rules of a game (see Ch. 1 and Ch. 4 for the further explanation of Piaget's theory). Because they understand that those rules serve them to play the game pleasurably and fairly, children freely engage in a discussion for the betterment of play and agree on the modification of some rules. This capability of children to evaluate the significance and efficacy of game rules and reformulate them enhances the joy of social activity and their confidence in personal capability. This cooperative activity of children can be a concrete example of well-being freedom in the conventional domain. In short, the existence and expansion of well-being freedom can be recognized and studied as an integral part of human development across the personal, conventional, and moral domains of social reasoning.

Agency freedom centers on the ideals to be realized and the objectives to achieve. Sen (1985) considers it to be broader than well-being freedom. Agency freedom transcends the welfare concerns of agents and sometimes contradicts them. Individuals can pursue social ideals and moral obligations while accepting the negative impacts on their own personal welfare. This idealistic feature of agency freedom is essential to moral judgments. This freedom may motivate individuals to concentrate on the realization of the common good which they surpass the personal concerns for their own well-being. It also resonates well with the sense of autonomy in the conventional domain. In this domain, persons may practice their agency freedom to develop social practices and create new norms for the facilitation of group functioning and the renewal of team spirit. In this sense, the conventional reasoning fundamentally goes beyond heteronomy (e.g., obedience to existing norms), as it envisions that both children and adults can be autonomous agents for the organization of interpersonal activities in the community. Finally, agency freedom can be realized in the personal domain in the individual search for the objectives related to personal likes and dislikes, not to social norms. These objectives cannot be established by others, but by the agents themselves. Their self-knowledge of their own uniqueness, tastes, and preferences is an essential component for the agency freedom of the personal domain. Therefore, agency freedom can be a useful concept to examine the meaning and role of freedom in the domains of social reasoning.

By explicating the relationship between the two types of freedom proposed by Sen (1985, 2006) and the three domains of social reasoning of Turiel (1983, 2002), I would like to confirm that morality requires both reasoning and freedom (cf. Williams, 2018).

Reasoning and freedom interact in the moral judgments of individuals. Without rational capacities, none can discern what is right or wrong. Without freedom, no moral judgments can be made in a responsible manner. Free rational humans possess the powers of thinking and imagining which enable them to discover principles and resources and formulate rules and orders in society. From a cognitive developmental perspective, it is entirely plausible that children's capacity for social reasoning about personal choices, autonomy, and civil liberties can be strongly influenced by the degree and quality of freedom that they experience in their relationships with others. Thus, it is worth pursuing a systematic understanding of the relationship between the domains of social reasoning and the types of freedom, and studying the research methods which can capture the dynamic interactions between freedom and reasoning.

6

Do Children Consider the Multifaceted Aspects of an Event?

In 2011, Chris Whitehead, a 13-year-old student, won Liberty's human rights award. He wore a skirt to his school because the school authorities did not allow boys to wear shorts in hot weather. It was not easy for male students to study in long trousers in this weather. He found a loophole in the school regulation on uniform, which obliged students to wear either trousers or a skirt without the specification of corresponding gender. He showed up at school in the skirt of his sister instead of his trousers in a sign of protest against a ban on shorts. (See Tomlinson, 2011.)

The story of Chris Whitehead reveals the capacity of an adolescent to reason about the complex realities of human interactions and make a judgment to challenge the pointless restriction and rigid mentality of the authorities. This episode touches various issues in the domain theory of social reasoning such as freedom of choice, the modification of tradition, and the wellness and right of adolescents. Most children and adolescents view the choice of clothes for schooling as a personal choice or conventional practice. They usually exercise a freedom of choice by judging themselves what to wear for their activities (i.e., the reasoning of the personal domain) unless they know that they should follow dress codes to attend certain institutional activities and gatherings (i.e., the reasoning of the conventional domain). By contrast, in the case of Chris Whitehead, his choice to wear a skirt wittingly manifested his intentions to promote the welfare of students (i.e., the reasoning of the moral domain). The moral implications of his action were well understood by his peers and neighbors and even awarded with a prestigious human rights prize. The case of a boy wearing a skirt to school can be an example of social reasoning about multifaceted events which

119

people can encounter in daily life. In this type of reasoning, it is necessary to review various aspects of a social practice or individual behavior in a specific context and systematically integrate them in the process of decision-making. In this chapter, I would like to discuss the studies on the reasoning of complex events from the social domain approach.

First, I will explain the nature of mixed domain and multifaceted events. They refer to the events which tend to ask individuals to include more than one domain of social reasoning in their judgments. Besides some typical events in an experimental setting such as physical violence in the moral domain, many events in real situations can make people consider simultaneously the diverse domains of reasoning. Starting with mixed domain events, I will examine how to analyze the complexity of social reasoning. Secondly, I will discuss the influence of the domain attribution of an event on decision-making. The domain attribution refers to the classification of domain(s) of the reasoning of an event based on the understanding of the nature of the event. As individuals do not always attribute one and the same domain to an event, they may make different decisions. Thirdly, I will examine the studies on the moral development of children and adolescents in two trajectories; developmental changes in the moral domain and in the coordination of domains. Especially, I will focus on the coordination of domains which suggests several unique findings and ideas on moral development according to social domain theory. Lastly, I will present and discuss the issue of moral consciousness in the context of moral education. After the review of developmental features in moral judgments, I will explain the significance of raising moral consciousness in the coordination of domains of social reasoning in multifaceted events.

Mixed Domain and Multifaceted Events

Smetana (1983) suggested that many judgments consist of more than one domain of social reasoning. Although some simple events are categorized in a single domain (e.g., helping a friend in need, as moral domain; having a break on Sunday, as conventional domain), quite a few events tend to make individuals consider more than one domain of social reasoning. For example, verbal offenses such as name-calling tend to be viewed as both moral and conventional transgressions. Name-calling can be considered to be a harmful and unjust insult and a violation of an ordinary manner of conversation in a society. The former reasoning belongs to the moral domain, and the latter, the conventional domain. Like this example of mixed domain events, individuals can think about both moral and non-moral concerns regarding various events in their daily lives.

Children and adolescents can identify multifaceted aspects of an event and integrate them in the process of reasoning and judgment across cultures. Hasebe et al. (2004) verified the presence of mixed domain events in the reasoning of both Japanese and American adolescents. For instance, "start dating," "watch a violent movie," and "get ear or nose pierced" were likely to be associated with the personal (i.e., individual choice about activities and friends), conventional (i.e., cultural practices and family rules), and/or prudential (i.e., concerns for safety and health) domains of reasoning (Hasebe et al., 2004, p. 820). Adolescents in the two different cultures thought that these issues involved both their own choices and parental controls. It is, thus, universal that human reasoning about personal interactions and social events may include multifaceted considerations from more than a single domain of social reasoning.

As Smetana (2006) wrote, "Many events or situations are multifaceted and entail overlapping concerns with morality, social conventions, prudence, pragmatics, or personal issues, sometimes in conflict with one another and sometimes in synchrony" (p. 123). Moreover, it should be noticed that a typical event of a domain can easily become complex and multifaceted when some conditions are added to the event. For example, "a boy hitting his friend" tends to be judged morally wrong due to the intrinsic harm of the violent behavior. However, it becomes complicated when it is known that the friend made the boy upset as he talked rudely about the mother of the boy. With this information, it becomes multifaceted. In this case, while the boy physically offended his friend, he was wounded psychologically by his friend. It means that psychological harm and physical violence become two relevant moral concerns for a judgment. As many social interactions are not always simple and straightforward but complex and intricate, it is necessary to understand how individuals think and judge concerning complex events by identifying and integrating different domains and multifaceted concerns of social reasoning.

The Coordination of Domains

Researchers with the social domain approach have studied how children and adolescents construct various forms of reasoning and coordinate them in their judgments when they face mixed domain events. The coordination of domains implies that individuals examine and identify the diverse domains and multiple concerns of a complex event, compare the weight or salience of one domain or concern to another, and make a final judgment in accordance with one aspect of the event considered more significant than others (see Smetana, 1983, 2006; Turiel, 1983, 2007). The coordination can be natural and smooth when the components of an event do not create conflicts. For example, the plan of a child to participate in a party at a friend's house (i.e., personal domain) is realized with the permission of the mother (i.e., conventional domain). However, the coordination of domains needs to be carefully examined when varying aspects of an event compete with one another for different conclusions. For example, children may decide not to follow the indication of a teacher to return home right after school in order to organize some fun activities among themselves in their secret place. In this example, the teacher's order can be considered conventional as it is a regulation of the authority and prudential as it concerns the safety of students, whereas the plan of the students can be considered conventional as they are playing as a group and personal as they are acting according to their preferences. When the components of a situation are not in synchrony, those involved in the situation should identify the components in conflict and compare the importance or prominence of one component compared to others in order to make a final decision.

Quite a few researchers have examined how children and adolescents make a judgment when a moral concern creates a conflict with non-moral considerations (Helwig, 1995; Hwang, 2013; Killen et al., 2002; Killen & Stangor, 2001). For example, Killen and Stanger (2001) examined how European American children and adolescents decide to include or exclude a peer in a hypothetical situation. In a straightforward situation, girls in a ballet club had to decide to accept or reject a boy, thinking that this activity was stereotypically for girls and some of them felt uncomfortable to accept him. In this situation, the vast majority of participants judged it appropriate to accept the boy. This signifies that they prioritized moral concerns such as equality and wellbeing over personal reasons such as one's preference regarding the gender of team members and/or conventional reasons such as the tradition of the club. However, the results were quite different when some information was added that there was only one post for a new member in the team and there were two candidates, a boy with poor skills and a girl with a high level of dancing performance. In this complex situation, about half of the children and about 80% of the adolescents endorsed the rejection of the boy from the ballet club, mainly by appealing to the good functioning of the club. This tendency signifies that adolescents weighed the importance of group functioning (i.e., a conventional concern) as greater than that of equality or psychological harm (i.e., a moral concern). From this type of study, it is revealed that most children and adolescents examine various aspects of a situation or incident and coordinate them to make a judgment.

The Domain of Reasoning and Decision-making

There are some common questions about social domain theory. "Does everybody attribute the same domain of reasoning to the same event?" "Does the attribution of the domain of the event influence one's decision-making?" Quite a few researchers have studied what domain of reasoning individuals adopt when they make a judgment regarding an event (see Turiel, 1983; Smetana, 2006). For example, Smetana (1981a) studied the reasoning and decision-making of female adolescents and young adults regarding abortion in the United States. She investigated which domain of reasoning was prominent in the thoughts of those young women about the abortion of a human fetus. One group of participants believed the fetus to be a human life from the moment of conception and viewed abortion as a moral issue. They believed that abortion is taking life and cannot be justified. Another group consisted of those who do not consider the fetus to be an equal human life. They thought that a genuine human life would start from the moment of birth and, thus, the abortion of a fetus was a personal issue which should be free from social regulations and moral values. The members of the first group were named moral reasoners, whereas those of the second group, personal reasoners. 25% of the young women were moral reasoners, whereas 35%, personal reasoners (Smetana, 1981a, pp. 217−218). Like this example, the judgments of individuals can vary by their knowledge, information, experience, context, and other factors.

According to the results of Smetana's study (1981a), the difference between young women in the comprehension of the nature of abortion influenced their decisions on unplanned pregnancies. 93% of the moral reasoners, who viewed abortion as immoral, made a choice to continue their pregnancies, whereas 93% of the personal reasoners, who viewed abortion as a personal choice, sought abortions (Smetana, 1981a, p. 220). Even though the pregnancy started without plan, those who captured the moral implications of the abortion of the fetus were highly likely to avoid abortion. This study demonstrated that people may not attribute the same domain of reasoning to the same event and, in turn, the attribution of domain to moral or personal affects one's decision-making. Thus, one's belief or knowledge regarding an event can influence the attribution of the domain of the event and the following judgment as well.

Furthermore, the acquisition of new information can affect one's decision. Hwang (2013) interviewed Korean children and adolescents to study how they make a decision when they invite peers to a birthday party. In the story of this study, the birthday child knows a biracial peer in the neighborhood. They are not close friends. However, the birthday child comes to know that the biracial peer wants to become his or her friend. Then, the participants were asked if and why it was all right for the child not to invite the biracial peer. More than 70% of the children answered that it was appropriate to invite the biracial peer to the birthday party. Although many would think that the choice of friends for play or social events depends on them (i.e., personal domain), the information about the desire of the biracial peer to have a friend induced them to focus on moral implications of the situation such as wellbeing (i.e., the psychological harm to the peer due to the decision of rejection) and human rights (i.e., the biracial peer should be treated equally). This result signifies that the reasoning of children tends to be flexible according to the level of knowledge and the type of information about situational components.

The Persistence of Moral Choice

Children and adolescents with a high level of moral consciousness are likely to reason and judge in accordance with moral concerns and maintain their moral choices despite new conflictual situational factors. In reality, it is not very rare in social interactions that individuals discern whether they should change their decisions when they obtain new information about the situations and events related to decisions. In this occasion of a new judgment or the renewal of an old decision, it can be assumed that the principal domain of reasoning for a judgment is associated with the possibility to change the initial judgment. I suggest that judgments with moral concerns may be more persistent than those with non-moral concerns when they encounter conflicts with the initial decisions. For instance, when individuals make a decision to help the poor based on moral reasons, they may continue their good works despite situational changes. However, those who do the same charitable work mainly as a cultural practice or the preservation of social membership, i.e., conventional reasons, may not persevere in the services when other concerns in their lives become obstacles to them.

Hwang (2011) studied how children and adolescents changed their initial judgments when additional information was given to them and found the persistent nature of moral choices compared to other judgments with non-moral justifications. In this study, there were participants who justified their initial decisions with moral reasons (e.g., welfare; "He should not hurt his friend."), not personal reasons (e.g., personal choice; "It is all right to invite only close friends to the birthday party) or conventional reasons (e.g., social tradition; "It is better to keep this tradition as it has some values."). Those who judged with moral justifications were less likely to change their judgments than other participants who justified with non-moral reasons when the contexts of judgment became rather complicated due to the new information which challenged the initial judgment. For instance, the majority of participants except the tenth graders (from 13.8 to 15.4 years) judge it appropriate to invite the biracial peer to the birthday party of the protagonist of the scenario. Then, it was told to the participants that the friends of the protagonist did not want the biracial peer to join the party and they were asked whether it is wrong to exclude the biracial peer. 72% of those who adopted moral reasoning did not change their initial decisions, whereas only 32% of those who justified with personal or conventional reasoning did not change them. A fourth-grade male kept his initial decision with his concern about the psychological wellbeing of the biracial peer, saying, "It is still better to invite Po (i.e., the biracial peer) to the party . . . they will come to know Po better and become friends as they get along together" (Hwang, 2011, p. 45). He persevered in his initial moral choice to include the peer by appealing to a right of the biracial peer to get a chance to play with peers. This finding implies that the original reasons for a decision matters when a situation becomes complex, and confirms that those who consider moral reasons more important than other considerations tend to continue to pursue their moral ideals.

The finding of Hwang (2011) regarding the relative persistency of moral choice resonates well with the study of Smetana (1981a) which revealed that women who viewed abortion as a moral issue tended to continue their unplanned pregnancies. Those young women probably had many other thoughts about their pregnancies along with moral concerns, but persevered in their initial judgments based on moral ideals. These tendencies indicate that moral choices are relatively persistent despite the tension with other non-moral concerns. However, this does not mean that moral reasoning is not flexible. Instead, individuals tend to apply their initial moral concerns to new contexts and integrate them with other emerging facts and considerations. In this process of new application, they are more likely to continue to prioritize their moral concepts over personal, conventional, and prudential concerns than those who initially have made non-moral choices.

Despite a human capability for moral reasoning and an enduring provision of moral justification in a conflictual situation, irrational and immoral incidents are overwhelmingly present in this world so that some researchers may become suspicious of human morality and deny the significance of rationality in moral judgments. Furthermore, as it is very challenging to understand the multifaceted components and complicated structure of social reasoning, some may say, "Human perception and cognition are more or less genetically conditioned like other animals" or "In the end, the irrational power of emotions takes over human decisions." Against these voices, Turiel (2007) emphasizes the rational nature of the moral judgments of children and adolescents. He perseveres in his premise that human beings are rational for his studies of moral development. From a social domain approach, individuals can make immoral decisions by prioritizing personal concerns over moral ideals such as justice, human rights, welfare, and freedom. Despite the moral failures of individuals, they are persistent in their nature as reasoning beings. Due to the presence of both morality and rationality in humans, we can hope for the conversion of immoral people. As long as they maintain their nature as rational beings, they have a possibility to raise their moral consciousness and convert to prioritize moral concerns over non-moral ones.

Two Trajectories of Moral Development

Moral reasoning develops together with the emergence of the conceptions of personal choice and privacy and the comprehension of the nature of social conventional norms (Nucci, 1983, 2013; Smetana, 2006; Turiel, 1983, 2002). While the stage model of Kohlberg (1969, 2008) envisioned that the development of morality would include the realm of conventional reasoning, the social domain approach delineates the developmental features of moral reasoning based on the distinction and coordination of domains. Thus, this domain approach induces the two trajectories of moral development. One deals with a development within the moral domain, and the other focuses on developmental changes in the coordination of domains. In the first trajectory, it was studied whether there are age differences in terms of justifications for moral judgments. Children and adolescents can make the same decision in a specific situation with different reasons and motivations. It is useful to review what has been found regarding developmental changes within the moral domain.[5] In the second trajectory, the main goal is to find some regularities in the coordination of children and adolescents between moral and non-moral reasoning. As studies with this scope have to deal with judgments on multifaceted issues in complex situations, it is challenging to integrate various results and produce clear indications about development. Still, the difference between children and adolescents has been confirmed in quite a few studies (see Hwang, 2013, Killen et al., 2002; Nucci & Turiel, 2009). By examining the two trajectories of moral development according to the social domain

---

[5] Developmental changes in the personal and conventional domains were studied by Nucci (1996) and Turiel (1983), respectively. However, not many research projects have been launched for these topics since the initial studies of Nucci and Turiel.

approach, it is expected to comprehend the realities of moral development and the roles of the moral domain in social reasoning.

Developmental Changes within the Moral Domain of Social Reasoning

Regarding the first trajectory of moral development, quite a few researchers of domain theory have focused on age-related changes in the moral reasons such as welfare, fairness, and human rights with which children justify their judgments. In a pioneering study of Smetana (1981b), it was found that preschool children began to make moral judgments over the events or incidents which entailed welfare concerns (e.g., physical harm due to hitting) more consistently than with other events which were associated mainly with fairness (e.g., sharing a toy in an equal manner). As the examples of behaviors like hitting showed explicitly the damage of a transgression, young children were able to answer that it was wrong to hit others because it hurt them. They steadily made this type of moral judgment according to their concerns about the welfare of others. It was, however, difficult for young children to make a judgment regarding a fair share of the toy. They often failed to reconcile their right to possess a toy with a necessity to share it with others in a certain condition (see Smetana, 2006, p. 124). Thus, it was suggested that justifications with welfare develop first and those with fairness follow within the moral domain of children's reasoning.

Since the initial study of Smetana (1981b), the understanding of the first trajectory of moral development turned out to be rather complex because of the finding that the use of justifications varies not simply by age but also by the diverse components of events and situations. For instance, Davidson et al. (1983) studied age variations in the organization of children's moral reasoning with a focus on the effect of one's familiarity with an event on their justifications for judgments. There were age-related differences among the three age groups of children; six, eight, and ten years. First of all, the older children were more likely than younger ones to justify their moral judgments with fairness for familiar events such as bullying. The incident was described as follows: "A boy bullies a group of children in the playground, pushing one off the top of the slide" (Davidson et al, 1983, p. 52). When the older children were asked why the bully did wrong, they tended to appeal to the necessity of an equilibrium between the common rights of children to use school facilities and their personal interests in enjoying them. The younger children, however, tended to judge it wrong as the bully hurt others (i.e., welfare). Secondly, the older children were more likely than younger children to justify their judgments with welfare regarding unfamiliar events such as a physician's duty: "An emergency room surgeon leaves his post due to boredom although there is no one to relieve him" (Davidson et al, 1983, p. 52). In the reasoning on this event, the older children tended to make a reference to the benefits and difficulties of patients or individuals other than the surgeon without dealing mainly with the duties of the protagonist. The younger children, however, could not capture consistently the moral implications of this incident. Thus, the influence of the factor "children's familiarity with events" on moral judgments implies that the experience and knowledge of children may affect the reasoning of children.

In addition, Hwang (2013) found age differences in the use of justifications in moral reasoning about the peer relationships. In this study, he asked Korean children and adolescents if and why it was appropriate for a biracial child to be banned from the swimming pool. While the vast majority judged it inappropriate not to allow the biracial child to swim in a public pool, they showed different tendencies by age in terms of justifications. Human rights were more frequently mentioned than other sorts of justifications by children and early adolescents (about 50% among the eight types of justifications), whereas those with fairness (69%) was widely used by middle adolescents (about 15 years of age). A justification with human rights implies an appeal to the rights of children to have equal opportunities for activities. An example of this justification is as follows: "Biracial people are the same humans like other Koreans. There should be no discrimination" (Hwang, 2011, p. 39). On the other hand, a justification with fairness refers to an appeal to make a decision without impartiality and treat individuals fairly according to reciprocity. For example, "Koreans can travel to other countries and eat foreign food there. Likewise, he should be allowed to do what he wants to do. It is fair to let him use the swimming pool" (Hwang, 2011, p. 39). While the justification with rights concentrates on the equal or common qualities of people without evaluating how a judgment is made, that with fairness points out the problem of discrimination between humans as well as the incorrect and ineffective aspects of a decision. From these results, it can be suggested that adolescents tend to reason in a broad and sophisticated manner more than children.

Despite certain significant findings regarding the development of reasoning in the moral domain, it is still difficult to clarify the developmental trajectory of reasoning in the moral domain. As reviewed above, children tend to start moral reasoning with welfare and then justify with fairness as they grow older (Davidson et al., 1983; Smetana, 1981b; Turiel, 1983). However, this emerging order between welfare and fairness reasoning may not be applied to all events and situations. As the study of Hwang (2013) deals mainly with judgments in the context of peer relationships, an appeal to human rights rather than welfare was commonly found among younger participants. Furthermore, young children could not make a distinction between moral and conventional domains when some incidents of judgments were complex or unfamiliar (Davidson et al., 1983; Hwang, 2013). In these cases, it was difficult to examine thoroughly age-related variations in the moral domain, as the boundary between moral and conventional reasoning was not clear.

By examining these mixed results, I do not think it plausible to identify a simple, universal order of stages, as in the stage theory of Kohlberg, in the moral domain of reasoning through the differentiations of justifications for judgments according to age. While young children with moral conceptions are adaptive to varying aspects and conditions in social interactions, they are not sufficiently knowledgeable about many complex events and incidents in their surroundings. On the one hand, their justifications for judgments may differ according to the theme or context. They may consider human rights first in a friendship context and welfare in a violent situation. It shows that their reasoning is flexible and adaptive to contexts. On the other hand, the complexity of a scenario or question in a study influences the capacity of children to distinguish convention from morality. Three- and four-year-old children can distinguish them in a simple, straightforward situation (Smetana, 1983; Turiel, 1983), whereas they cannot in an unfamiliar, complex situation (Davidson et al., 1983; Hwang, 2013). This contrast may answer why Kohlberg could not find the differentiation between post-conventional and conventional judgments among children. As he adopted a highly complicated story like the Heinz Dilemma, children under 13 years of age might not be able to show their capacity for moral reasoning. Nevertheless, there is a common finding of the studies regarding development in the moral domain, i.e., the age-related increase of fairness reasoning between children and adolescents. It implies that children tend to focus on the well-being or rights of an individual, whereas adolescents are likely to review the quality of the judgment process together with the welfare and rights of related people.

Developmental Changes in the Coordination of Domains

Children and adolescents grow in their capacity for the coordination of domains (Helwig, 1995; Hwang, 2013; Smetana, 1983; Turiel, 1983, 2002). When they encounter multifaceted events, they examine the various aspects of events and think about coordinating them by differentiating between moral and non-moral considerations in their reasoning, and decide which considerations they prioritize. From the initial studies of the social domain approach, the capacity of coordination in the reasoning of children over hypothetical conflicts between social rules and moral reasoning can be indirectly observed. For instance, the majority of children did not think appropriate the school policy which allowed them to hit one another (Weston & Turiel, 1980). This implies that children identified and coordinated the two components of the situation, which were the observance of school policy (i.e., conventional) and the problems of hitting (i.e., moral). They tended to think the moral concern of the situation was more important than the conventional practice of the school in this hypothetical situation, and rejected the policy which would make them hurt one another. Even young children have a capacity to identify the competing concerns of different domains and coordinate them to make a judgment when the contexts of judgments are not too complicated.

Researchers of domain theory have examined whether children would reveal age differences in terms of the capacity of coordination. For instance, Nucci and Turiel (2009) demonstrated the particular features of the group of adolescents at around 14 years of age in comparison with younger and older participants in their coordination of moral reasoning with non-moral reasoning in various complex situations. In one of the scenarios (Nucci & Turiel, 2009), the protagonist needs $10 more for an activity with friends and cannot find a way to earn it. In a bus, a passenger drops a $10 bill and nobody but the protagonist observes it. The protagonist should decide whether to take the bill secretly and use it for the activity or tell the passenger to pick it up. This scenario was intended to examine whether the participants make a moral choice by giving priority to moral considerations (i.e., helping the passenger pick up the bill) over conventional or personal reasons (i.e., the importance of group activity or personal choice). From this study, it was found that young adolescents, more than children and old adolescents, were prone to endorse an immoral act. Thus, no linear progression or regression of a certain type of coordination by age was found in the empirical studies from the social domain perspective.

In the past, some stage theories like Kohlberg's moral development theory are based on the assumption of the linear progression of a certain capability and tendency by age. Kohlberg (1969, 1971) certainly thought that adolescents tend to be more advanced in moral reasoning than children. Unlike the assumption of stage theory, Nucci and Turiel (2009) suggested a U-shaped pattern of developmental trajectory in the coordination of domains. The frequency of morally-led judgments tended to be high in childhood and low in early adolescents, and became higher in late adolescents. In other words, the tendency of non-moral choice arrives at a peak at the period of early adolescence and diminishes afterwards (see Nucci et al., 1996). It can be assumed that young adolescents are likely to enlarge vigorously the range of personal choices, view their exercise of freedom in various contexts as the realization of inviolable human rights, and subordinate moral concerns for the welfare of others to their own personal freedom and choices in the decision-making process (see Nucci, 2013; Nucci et al., 1996; Smetana, 2006). Due to this particularity of young adolescents, the developmental trajectory of the coordination of domains seems to create a curvilinear pattern by age, not a linear pattern of progress in the course of moral development.

The Influence of Peers on the Coordination of Middle Adolescents

Hwang (2011) found a particular feature of adolescents in their coordination between personal reasoning and conventional reasoning. That is, the opinions of peers were influential on their decisions. For instance, the tenth graders (from 13.8 to 15.4 years) in South Korea were less likely to endorse the invitation of a biracial peer to a birthday party than the younger participants. They tended to support the personal decision of the protagonist to invite only intimate friends to the party and exclude the biracial peer who was not close to him or her. According to the results of the study, only 28% of them thought that it was wrong to exclude the biracial peer from the party. It denotes that the majority of the adolescents might not invite the biracial peer to their personal gatherings among close friends even though they knew the possible disappointment or loneliness of the peer. However, this tendency changed considerably in the following situation in which it was made known in addition that the friends of the protagonist wanted to have the biracial peer at the party. 67% of the tenth graders judged the invitation of the peer as appropriate. Although the two other groups of younger participants (from 8.3 to 12.5 years) did not show any significant changes due to the introduction of the new situational factor (i.e., the contrasting opinions of the friends to the decision of the protagonist), the tenth graders showed a drastic change from 28% of the endorsement of inclusion to 67% when they came to know the opinion of the friends of the protagonist. It was, thus, suggested that the impact of peer pressure as a part of conventional reasoning tended to be significant enough to change the initial judgments of Korean adolescents which were based on personal preferences.

According to Steinberg and Monahan (2007), the resistance to peer pressure among middle adolescents tends to be lower than among early or late adolescents regarding antisocial behaviors. On the one hand, this developmental trajectory is apparently similar to the pattern which Nucci and Turiel (2009) found regarding the low frequency of moral choice of early adolescents. Both results show a U-shape pattern in the course of development in adolescence. On the other hand, the weak resistance to peer pressure in the study of Steinberg and Monahan (2007) resonates with the ready acceptance of peers' suggestions in that of Hwang (2011). Both studies clearly indicate the particular impact of friends and peers on the judgments and behaviors of middle adolescents. In terms of the developmental features of transitional periods, both personal freedom and peer pressure tend to increase from late childhood to middle adolescence and decrease after middle adolescence.

The non-linear trajectory of the development of coordination of domains of social reasoning denotes a need to delve into the inner process of judgments in early and middle adolescence. While acknowledging as features of this period the expansion of personal freedom, the confusion between personal freedom and human rights (Nucci & Turiel, 2009), and susceptibility to the suggestions of peers (Hwang, 2011), I want to be careful in interpreting the significance of peer relationships and activities with friends. In this period of human development, the sense of belonging to a group of friends can be more precious and essential than in other periods of development and can affect significantly the psychological wellness of young adolescents. Although group activities based on personal preferences do not seem to convey explicitly moral values or prudential concerns, adolescents may perceive them in a different manner and view them as indispensable components of their wellbeing and social life. It should be verified whether the relationship with friends possess particular moral implications for them and how the importance of friendship changes during adolescence.

Relationship between Judgment and Action

The consistency between judgment and action has been an essential issue in the studies of moral development and education. Many assumed that moral judgments are not always coupled with morally correct behaviors. Especially in a complex situation, this kind of discrepancy between moral judgment and action seems to be often observed in daily life. In the studies of Nucci and Turiel (2009), a good number of adolescents decided to take the money of another person to participate in a group activity. They made this decision, even though they knew that any acquisition of the money of another person with no consent was not morally correct. Their decision was not consistent with their moral reasoning. Like this example, individuals may not follow their moral judgments due to some personal or conventional reason. In this case, their actions are not consistent with their moral judgments. In other words, there can be discrepancies between moral concerns and final judgments in the coordination of various thoughts. These discrepancies, however, do not signify that people behave without rationality or are driven by emotions (cf. Haidt, 2001). In the process of the coordination of domains, the final judgments of individuals may or may not prioritize moral concerns vis-à-vis non-moral social concerns. There is no absolute rule in reality which prescribes that personal or conventional concerns should yield to moral ones. Since moral reasoning is not the unique and global mode of the human thinking process, individuals need to examine other thoughts, sentiments, and concerns which interact with moral thoughts.

It is questionable if the final judgments of individuals are inconsistent with their actions. When adolescents decided to take the $ 10 bill of the passenger on the bus, their conventional reasoning about the importance of the event with friends, not moral reasoning about the inappropriate use of another person's money, corresponded to the decision. In this case, the consistency between the final judgment and action is preserved, even though the judgment is not morally right. It implies that judgment and action in an individual are in synchrony. As the discrepancy between moral reasoning and behavior signifies that non-moral concerns are prioritized over moral ones in the coordination, this discrepancy is compatible with the consistency between judgment and action. From the social domain approach, individuals do not stop the use of their rationality in their decision-making process. Individuals are thinking rationally, even though their decisions can be neither moral nor logical. Most people do not always make morally correct and logically valid judgments. Some rationalize their poor decisions and unethical behaviors. Nevertheless, people are rational thinkers and behave according to their judgments, based on the coordination of various factors in a given situation.

The Role of Emotion in a Process of Coordination

The process of coordination between domains reveals the crucial role of emotion in social reasoning. To explain it, I would like to apply the idea of Piaget (1954, 1966). Basically, emotions, which include motivations, are the estimable source of energy and parallel to the structures of cognition (Piaget, 1954). Then, it can be thought that every single cognitive component has a certain amount of emotion. In the situation where two thoughts are polarized and competing with each other, it can be easily assumed that one thought with a higher level of energy (i.e., motivation or emotional value) would lead to a final decision over against the other thought with a lower level of energy. In the studies of coordination, "being salient" or "weighing more or less" has been a common description of the evaluation of the domains to be coordinated in a decision-making process (see Smetana, 2006; Turiel, 2007). Individuals prioritize moral concerns over non-moral ones when they perceive the moral concerns as more salient or as weighing more than the non-moral ones. From Piaget's approach (1954), it can be suggested that the coordination of domains is associated with the evaluation of the strength of emotion/motivation of each concern or domain. When a concern in the moral domain possesses a higher level of emotion than other concerns, individuals are likely to judge and behave according to the moral concern. From this assumption, it might be said that the role of emotion is decisive in the process of coordination as the energy levels which accompany cognitive components can decide the direction of the conclusion (see Turiel, 2006a, 2006b).

Although the explanation, that an individual makes a final judgment with the domain or concern more salient than others in the process of coordination, is generally acceptable, there can be some complications when there is a conflict between one's will and emotional reactions. For example, those who are recovering from addictions can remain in abstinence while they are still craving for addictive substances. In this case, the desire for drugs can often be more salient than any other emotional reactions and motivational forces. Nevertheless, the recovering addict may resist the strong temptation of the drug and continue to live in abstinence, suggesting that the final judgment can suppress the tempting thought of relapse when it is associated with a firm will to stay sober. In this case, it is somewhat difficult to explain the process of coordination only with the salience of an emotional reaction.

For the clarification of the nature of this case, I resort to the idea of Piaget about affective structures. Although emotions as energy do not have any mental structures, unlike cognition, certain emotions can adopt the structures of cognition and become affective structures at a high level of development (Piaget, 1954). Some sorts of will or moral feelings can be assumed as emotions or motivations with structures. In the example of abstinence from a substance, the will to be sober as a mental structure can function as the mechanism of inhibition. It becomes like a dam to contain the powerful emotional flow attached to a relapse so that the recovering addict may make a final judgment to continue the resolution of abstinence (cf. Piaget, 1954, pp. 61 − 65). By adopting the ideas of Piaget on affective structures, it would be possible to envision theoretically the roles of emotions which go beyond the magnitude of energy attached to a cognitive structure or the perceived salience of an intellectual component. As Piaget carried out no experiments on the role of emotion, it is difficult to find proper evidence for his assumption. It is also challenging to conduct empirical studies on the roles of emotions in the coordination of domains, as they are not easily measured in a direct manner but may be inferred from related factors. Nevertheless, the ideas of Piaget on the relationship between emotion and cognition would be valuable for the studies on the roles of emotion in the coordination of domains.

Raising Moral Consciousness

In the end, I would like to discuss the issue of raising moral consciousness as an essential aspect of moral education in light of the social domain theory. In the history of the modern world, questions about an effective moral education have not encountered many good answers. Moral education projects based on the stage theory of Kohlberg did not reveal any significant effects and other attempts such as character education have not been very promising (Nucci & Turiel, 2009). Therefore, it seems realistic not to expect the creation of a moral education program which is exceptionally effective and easily applicable. Along the same line, researchers with the social domain approach have not suggested any master plan of moral education, but addressed some important issues. Thus, I will focus on the issue of moral consciousness in the process of coordination and its implications for moral education.

According to Nucci and Turiel (2009), "The emphasis of moral education would be upon engaging students in the process of bringing the recognized complexities of multifaceted situations into coordinating with morality" (p. 158). This point can be analyzed into the two types of capacities which are necessary for a coordination of domains. First, it is important for individuals to recognize moral implications in a multifaceted situation. Without this identification, regardless of whether it is implicit or explicit, there is no way to make a moral judgment. Secondly, it is necessary to coordinate moral concerns with other concerns without losing or devaluing the significance of moral concerns. Individuals with a poor capacity of coordination tend to fail to integrate some important domains or considerations in their decision-making process (Nucci et al., 2013). These two types of capacities constitute the concept of moral consciousness. It refers to a rational operation to find the implications of the moral domain in a particular context and coordinate them with other concerns from non-moral domains. When moral education helps children and adolescents to think about an event or behavior in terms of justice, welfare, and human rights, it may raise their moral consciousness.

When young students are well equipped with ethical knowledge and scientific information, it can be effective to enhance the capacity of students to capture moral implications in their daily lives. For example, washing one's hands in an ordinary context may have personal and prudential implications. However, this simple behavior can have a different significance during the Covid-19 pandemic. It certainly includes the dimension of moral reasoning especially regarding the welfare of people. When students understand that they can be infected or infect others by their polluted hands and seriously harm themselves and others, they are ready to acknowledge that their behaviors convey serious moral implications. If they do not recognize the moral value of cleaning their hands in the pandemic, based on scientific knowledge about infection, they may not behave as morally mature persons.

In terms of the method of education or discipline, moral consciousness may not be successfully raised by power-assertive educational measures but by induction or reasoning. Returning to the example of hand-washing, educators can decide to punish students when they do not wash their hands. Considering the frequent needs of washing hands and the limited capacity of monitoring by teachers compared to the number of students, it might not be very effective and would hardly help the moral reasoning of students. Instead, teachers could explain the nature of infection, the importance of personal hygiene including washing hands, and the consequences of the failure to practice preventive measures (cf. JTBC News, 2020.) This type of induction can help students become autonomous, prudent, conscientious, and ethical. Like this example, when they understand logically why certain actions and rules are important for the welfare of others and social justice, instead of being forced to obey them without an understanding, students can make a sound judgment with their moral consciousness. Thus, adults need to guide children and adolescents gradually to think about the multifaceted aspects of incidents, discern the moral implications of the incidents, and coordinate them with non-moral components in a particular context.

7

Conclusion: Crossing the Boundary of Conventional Morality

A 27-year-old policeman—Tha Peng— crossed the border between Myanmar and India on February 29, 2021. When his superior officer ordered him to shoot to death peaceful protesters in Myanmar, he refused the order, resigned from his position, left his family behind, and fled into India (Ghoshal, 2021). What he really crossed was not simply a geographical boundary, but the barrier of conventional morality. Kohlberg (1969, 1971) indicated that individuals on the level of conventional morality obey the rules and regulations of authority figures and believe that their obedience makes them moral. This type of attitude and judgment is not genuinely ethical because the foundation of morality does not consist of laws and regulations but universal principles such as human rights and social justice. When morality is defined by human conventions, it has to suffer instability and inconsistency because state laws or cultural norms as social artifacts are subject to modification and reformulation by the members of a society. Furthermore, some laws or regulations such as the orders of Myanmar's military junta do not protect but harm the majority of people who follow the voice of their conscience. Many laws regarding industries also tend to prioritize the benefits of individuals with power and money over those of ordinary working-class people. By remaining within the boundary of conventions, human beings are hardly guaranteed to be authentically moral. On quite a few occasions, such as the example of the young policeman from Myanmar, individuals can find a way to become moral only by rejecting the conventional morality, i.e., obedience to the orders of authority figures in a society. Thus, human beings could maintain their dignity as moral agents and fully realize social ideals only by opening themselves up to seek to transcend the boundary of convention.

In the academic field of child development, Turiel (1983) crossed the boundary of Kohlberg's stage theory of moral development. Whereas Kohlberg thought that children under 13 years of age could not differentiate morality from convention and remained in the level of conventional or pre-conventional morality, Turiel and his colleagues (1983, Smetana, 1983) found that four- or five-year-old children could distinguish between moral failures (e.g., hitting another child) and conventional transgressions (e.g., not to place toys back to original places after having played with them) and understand that their judgments on moral issues do not change even if there are no rules on them (e.g., it is wrong to hit a friend even if there is no rule to prohibit it). Thus, the notion of conventional morality cannot continue to be present in the social domain theory of Turiel. Instead, morality and convention are to be regarded as two independent thinking systems of social reasoning. His ideas about the distinction between moral and conventional domains correspond to the theories of some prominent philosophers such as Gewirth (1978) and Rawls (1971) on morality (see Turiel, 1983, pp. 35−36). These philosophers suggested that moral judgments should not be subjected to the authority or practices of social institutions. Fundamentally, morality is not based on the laws of states but on the inviolable rights of human beings. Although it is true that most governments try to realize moral and social ideals in their legal systems, their efforts cannot remove or aim at eliminating the fundamental gap between law and morality. Thus, the amalgamation of convention and morality such as conventional morality (i.e., morality equals following laws) cannot be justified both empirically and theoretically.

The life of people can be disgraceful and inhumane when they close themselves within the boundary of conventions. Particularly, children, adolescents, and vulnerable adults can become the victims of some social practices when they are not allowed to exercise freedom but constrained by the authority of families, religions, and societies that refuse to go beyond the cultural barriers of their organizations. For example, *trokosi* is a traditional practice in some tribes in West Africa where parents offer their young virgin daughters as the slaves of the authority figures of religious shrines to expiate the sins of a family member (Dzansi & Biga, 2014). In these places, the human rights of young girls are seriously violated in the name of religious traditions. Like this example, there are quite a few traditional practices which violate human rights. Certainly, many nations try to establish certain laws to identify and prevent some problematic cultural practices. The absence of related regulations about the rights of women or children, however, can never be an excuse for any violation of human rights. Thus, individuals should not stop their search to discern the moral implications of conventional practices and go beyond the boundary of conventions. Despite certain variations in capacities for moral judgments, most young and old people are able to judge what is wrong and right regarding ethically relevant issues such as abuse and violence.

The social domain approach to social reasoning does not consider every single judgment of right and wrong in human interactions to be moral. There are different qualities in judgments of right or wrong. Namely, judgments based on human rights, welfare, justice, and other related values belong to the moral domain, whereas those for the functioning of groups and the facilitation of daily interactions, to the conventional domain of social reasoning. Individuals who do not comprehend or who ignore the co-existence and distinction of the moral and conventional domains may wrongly evaluate transgressions in cultural and conventional norms as moral issues. For instance, some old people condemn the nontraditional outfits and decorations of young people as a moral failure or a sign of moral decay. This kind of moral condemnation of cultural or conventional issues misses the mark (see Turiel, 2002). For a rationally valid judgment, it is essential to avoid the confusion of domains. It is particularly problematic when moral relevancy is given to a conventional or private operation.

Furthermore, the errors of conventional morality cannot be exonerated as the unavoidable consequences of moral development. If the ideas of Kohlberg (1969, 1971) on the invariant stages of moral development are correct, individuals cannot reach the level of post-conventional morality—authentic moral judgments based on universal values and principles—without passing the level of conventional morality. According to this logic, individuals at the level of conventional morality have to commit the errors of obeying the immoral laws because they believe that morality equals following the laws and are not capable of reasoning according to moral values. However, Kohlberg's theory of the invariant stages of morality is proved to be invalid because the various studies of Turiel and his colleagues in different cultures (Turiel, 1983, 2002; Smetana, 2006) have confirmed that even young children can differentiate morality from convention. It signifies that children, adolescents, and adults are able to make moral judgments based on social ideals such as fairness and human rights. Thus, individuals should be responsible for their failures to follow unethical conventions and not to disobey inhuman cultural practices.

People cannot go beyond the boundary of convention to realize moral values without freedom. Above all, freedom is the core aspect of human rights. According to Article 19 of the Universal Declaration of Human Rights, "Everyone has the right to freedom of opinion and expression; this right includes freedom to hold opinions without interference and to seek, receive and impart information and ideas through any media and regardless of frontiers" (Universal Declaration of Human Rights, 1948). The value of freedom is not arbitrary or alterable by cultures, but fundamental and significant to all humans. Furthermore, studies on the moral development of children in the field of psychology demonstrated that children and adolescents unmistakably acknowledge the importance of freedom in their reasoning (Turiel, 2006b, p. 10). They value their freedom of choice and want adults to respect it.

It is a grave mistake in moral education if parental disciplinary practices aim at removing the freedom of children. The excessive control of freedom can result in many complications in the development of children and adolescents. Particularly, the extreme type of parental discipline which stifles the children's freedom of choice can leave serious marks on their personalities. Nucci (1996) presented a clinical case of a girl whose freedom of choice was seriously limited by her mother. She was not able to realize her freedom even in the selection of dress and food. Unfortunately, the girl suffered psychological problems such as depression and eating disorder and found it difficult to create friendships with peers. This case indicates that adults should understand and endorse the quest of children for freedom. This desire for freedom can never be erased in the heart of moral and rational agents.

In the psyche of free human beings, they can go beyond their experience. With freedom and rationality, they are able to imagine doing what they have neither done nor observed and realize their imagination in their social interactions. This capacity to transcend the boundary of their lived experience facilitates the realization of moral ideals. For instance, on December 1, 1955 Rosa Parks as an African American exercised her freedom of choice in a city bus. She made a decision to refuse the order of the bus driver to yield her seat to a white passenger (Parks & Haskins, 1999). It was not an arbitrary choice but an intentional moral operation of a free human being, which transcended the boundary of personal choices defined by conventions. In those days, African Americans could take a seat only in a designated section in a bus. Although Rosa Parks took her seat in the "colored" section in the bus on that day, the bus driver extended the "white" section as Caucasian passengers increased and she was asked to move to a newly defined "colored" section. She did not follow the order of the driver but remained in the seat that she had chosen. She was arrested by the police and her arrest ignited the movement for the abolition of Montgomery's segregation laws. Later she was called "the mother of the freedom movement" ("Rosa Parks," 2020). She transcended internally her realm of experience (i.e., for the first time she opted for being arrested instead of giving up her seat) and externally the boundary of her free choice and societal laws (i.e., the segregation laws did not permit her to remain in the "white" section). She exercised her freedom as a rational agent to achieve the ideals of human dignity and equality. Thus, history remembers her remarkable courage to confront inhumane legal and conventional practices.

The moral reasoning of free humans refuses to be inactive, restricted, and silent. The moral domain of social reasoning is not conceptualized to limit human morals to a list of good conducts. Instead, the discovery of this domain demonstrates the unique dynamic features of moral judgments. Basically, any written laws or book of ethics cannot fully capture the universal moral ideals of humanity and reinforce people to obey them. With or without recalling the existing norms of a society or the orders of authority figures, both children and adults can appreciate the values of justice, welfare, and human rights and make value-laden judgments. In other words, the dynamic nature of moral judgments does not allow humans to confine morals within a fixed format. When moral ideals and principles are codified, they become conventions and lose the vitality of human morals. Thus, humans should discern the moral implications of events and find a way to coordinate them with non-moral concerns in their decisions and behaviors. Ethical considerations should not be kept exclusively in the moral domain but let flow over the boundary of the domain to integrate with other concerns so that people may make realistic decisions to realize social ideals.

Nam-Ju Kim, a Korean poet wrote a poem about hope, saying "Brethren, I wish you do not seek justice in the court" (2014). I may wish humans do not seek morals in law books. I do not mean that all individuals are morally mature enough to live peacefully together without any legal reinforcements. But I do wish to imply that humans do not become moral by knowing what is written in books. Although I have written much about moral development, I do not believe that any theories possess power to make human beings moral. Even though some intellectuals have developed an advanced capacity for moral reasoning, there is no guarantee that their decisions will be moral, because they may not prioritize moral considerations over non-moral ones. Without exception, thus, those who desire to live up to social ideals are invited to place themselves in the tension which the vital nature of morality creates. In a final step, seeking to leave an answer to the question "How can humans become moral?", I would say: Certainly, human beings can become truly moral by consistently raising their moral consciousness and continuously crossing the boundaries of conventions.

References

Abbot, P., Abe, J., Alcock, J., Alizon, S., Alpedrinha, J. A. C., Andersson, M., Andre, J. B., van Baalen, M., Balloux, F., Balshine, S., Barton, N., Beukeboom, L. W., Biernaskie, J. M., Bilde, T., Borgia, G., Breed, M., Brown, S., Bshary, R., Buckling, A., ... Zink, A. (2011). Inclusive fitness theory and eusociality. *Nature, 471*(7339). https://doi.org/10.1038/nature09831

Ackerman, B. P., Abe, J. A., & Izard, C. E. (1988). Differential emotions theory and emotional development: Mindful of modularity. In M. F. Mascolo & S. Griffin (Eds.), *What develops in emotional development?* (pp. 53–84). Plenum Press.

Arsenio, W., & Lover, A. (1995). Children's conceptions of sociomoral affect: Happy victimizers, mixed emotions, and other expectancies. In M Killen & D. Hart (Eds.), *Morality in everyday life: Developmental perspectives* (pp. 87–128). Cambridge University Press.

Baum, P., Schmid, R., Ittrich, C., Rust, W., Fundel-Clemens, K., Siewert, S., Baur, M., Mara, L., Gruenbaum, L., Heckel, A., Eils, R., Kontermann, R. E., Roth, G. J., Gantner, F., Schnapp, A., Park, J. E., Weith, A., Quast, K., & Mennerich, D. (2010). Phenocopy – A strategy to qualify chemical compounds during hit-to-lead and/or lead optimization. *PLOS ONE, 5*(12), e14272. https://doi.org/10.1371/journal.pone.0014272

Baumrind, D. (1966). Effects of authoritative parental control on child behavior. *Child Development, 37*(4), 887–907. https://doi.org/10.2307/1126611

Baumrind, D. (1989). Rearing competent children. In W. Damon (Ed.), *New directions for child development: Adolescent health and social behavior* (pp. 349–378). Jossey-Bass.

Baumrind, D. (1991). The influence of parenting style on adolescent competence and substance use. *The Journal of*

Early Adolescence, 11(1), 56–95.
https://doi.org/10.1177/0272431691111004

Baumrind, D. (2005). Patterns of parental authority and adolescent autonomy. *New Directions for Child and Adolescent Development, 108*, 61–69. https://doi.org/10.1002/cd.128

Baumrind, D. (2013). Is a pejorative view of power assertion in the socialization process justified? *Review of General Psychology, 17*, 420. https://doi.org/10.1037/a0033480

Baumrind, D., Larzelere, R. E., & Owens, E. B. (2010). Effects of preschool parents' power assertive patterns and practices on adolescent development. *Parenting: Science and Practice, 10*(3), 157–201. https://doi.org/10.1080/15295190903290790

Bloom, P. (2013). *Just babies: The origins of good and evil.* Crown.

Bloom, P., & Wynn, K. (2016). What develops in moral development? In D. Barner & A. S. Baron (Eds.), *Core knowledge and conceptual change* (pp. 347–364). Oxford University Press.

Brown, T., & Kozak, A. (1988). Emotion and the possibility of psychologists entering into heaven. In M. F. Mascolo & S. Griffin (Eds.), *What develops in emotional development?* (pp. 135–155). Plenum Press.

Choe, S. Y., & Min, K.H. (2011). Who makes utilitarian judgments? The influences of emotions on utilitarian judgments. *Judgment and Decision Making, 6*(7), 580–592. http://journal.sjdm.org/11/11904/jdm11904.pdf

Chong, K. (2008). Classical Confucianism (II): Meng Zi and Xun Zi. In B. Mou (Ed.), *History of Chinese philosophy* (pp. 189–208). Routledge.

Cowell, J. M., & Decety, J. (2015). Precursors to morality in development as a complex interplay between neural, socioenvironmental, and behavioral facets. *Proceedings of the National Academy of Sciences, 112*(41), 12657–12662. https://doi.org/10.1073/pnas.1508832112

Damasio, A. R. (2003). *Looking for Spinoza: Joy, sorrow, and the feeling brain.* Mariner Books.

References

Damon, W. (1988). *Moral child: Nurturing children's natural moral growth*. Free Press.

Darwin, C. (1874). *The descent of man*. Penguin Classics.

Davidson, P., Turiel, E., & Black, A. (1983). The effect of stimulus familiarity on the use of criteria and justifications in children's social reasoning. *British Journal of Developmental Psychology, 1*(1), 49–65. https://doi.org/10.1111/j.2044-835X.1983.tb00543.x

De Waal, F. (2009). *Primates and philosophers: How morality evolved*. Princeton University Press.

Decety, J., & Howard, L. H. (2013). A neurodevelopmental perspective on morality. In Melanie Killen & J. Smetana (Eds.), *Handbook of moral development* (2nd ed., pp. 454–474). Psychology Press.

Decety, J., Michalska, K. J., & Kinzler, K. D. (2012). The contribution of emotion and cognition to moral sensitivity: A neurodevelopmental study. *Cerebral Cortex, 22*(1), 209–220. https://doi.org/10.1093/cercor/bhr111

Dzansi, D. Y., & Biga, P. (2014). Trokosi' - Slave of a fetish: An empirical study. *Studies of Tribes and Tribals, 12*(1), 1–8. https://doi.org/10.1080/0972639X.2014.11886681

Eisenberg, N. (2002). Distinctions among various modes of empathy-related reactions: A matter of importance in humans. *Behavioral and Brain Sciences, 25*(1), 33–34. https://doi.org/10.1017/S0140525X02350015

Eisenberg, N., Eggum, N. D., & Di Giunta, L. (2010). Empathy-related responding: Associations with prosocial behavior, aggression, and intergroup relations. *Social Issues and Policy Review, 4*(1), 143–180. https://doi.org/10.1111/j.1751-2409.2010.01020.x

Erikson, E. H. (1993). *Childhood and society*. Norton.

Fang, T. H. (1981). *Chinese philosophy: Its spirit and its development*. Linking Publishing.

Feng, Y. (1975). *Storia della filosofia cinese*. Arnaldo Mondadori Editore.

Fletcher, G. E., Warneken, F., & Tomasello, M. (2012).
Differences in cognitive processes underlying the
collaborative activities of children and chimpanzees.
Cognitive Development, 27(2), 136–153.
https://doi.org/10.1016/j.cogdev.2012.02.003

Free Speech Movement | UC Berkeley Library. (n.d.). Retrieved
June 25, 2020, from
https://www.lib.berkeley.edu/libraries/bancroft-library/oral-
history-center/projects/fsm

Freud, S. (1923). *The ego and the id.* W.W. Norton & Co.

Freud, S. (1930). *Civilization and its discontents.* W.W. Norton &
Co.

Freud, S. (1974). *The standard edition of the complete
psychological works of Sigmund Freud* (A. Freud, Ed.; J.
Strachey, Trans.). Hogarth Press.

Gesell, A. (1940). *The first five years of life: A guide to the study of
the preschool child.* Harper and Brothers.

Gewirth, A. (1978). *Reason and morality.* University of Chicago
Press.

Ghoshal, D. (2021, March 10). Exclusive: "Shoot till they are dead"
- Some Myanmar police say fled to India after refusing
orders. *Reuters.* https://www.reuters.com/article/us-
myanmar-politics-india-exclusive-idUSKBN2B12U2

Goldin, P. R. (2018). Xunzi. In E. N. Zalta (Ed.), *The Stanford
encyclopedia of philosophy* (Fall 2018 ed.). Metaphysics
Research Lab, Stanford University.
https://plato.stanford.edu/archives/fall2018/entries/grrnexun
zi/

Gordon, A. M., & Browne, K. W. (2013). *Beginnings & beyond:
Foundations in early childhood education.* Cengage
Learning.

Graham, J., Haidt, J., Koleva, S., Motyl, M., Iyer, R., Wojcik, S. P.,
& Ditto, P. H. (2013, January 1). Moral foundations theory:
The pragmatic validity of moral pluralism. *Advances in
Experimental Social Psychology, 47,* 55–130.
https://doi.org/10.1016/B978-0-12-407236-7.00002-4

Greene, J. D. (2009). Dual-process morality and the personal/impersonal distinction: A reply to McGuire, Langdon, Coltheart, and Mackenzie. *Journal of Experimental Social Psychology, 45*(3), 581–584. doi:10.1016/j.jesp.2009.01.003

Greene, J. D., Nystrom, L. E., Engell, A. D., Darley, J. M., & Cohen, J. D. (2004). The neural bases of cognitive conflict and control in moral judgment. *Neuron, 44*(2), 389–400. https://doi.org/10.1016/j.neuron.2004.09.027

Greene, J. D., Morelli, S. A., Lowenberg, K., Nystrom, L. E., & Cohen, J. D. (2008).
Cognitive load selectively interferes with utilitarian moral judgment. *Cognition, 107*(3), 1144–1154. https://doi.org/10.1016/j.cognition.2007.11.004

Greene, J. D., Sommerville, R. B., Nystrom, L. E., Darley, J. M., & Cohen, J. D. (2001). An fMRI investigation of emotional engagement in moral judgment. *Science, 293*(5537), 2105–2108. https://doi.org/10.1126/science.1062872

Griffin, S., & Mascolo, M. F. (1998). On the nature, development, and functions of emotions. In Michael F. Mascolo & S. Griffin (Eds.), *What develops in emotional development?* (pp. 3–27). Springer.

Grusec, J. E., Chaparro, M. P., Johnston, M., & Sherman, A. (2013). The development of moral behavior from a socialization perspective. In Melanie Killen & J. Smetana (Eds.), *Handbook of moral development* (2nd ed., pp. 113–134). Psychology Press.

Haidt, J. (2001). The emotional dog and its rational tail: A social intuitionist approach to moral judgment. *Psychological Review, 108*(4), 814–834. https://doi.org/10.1037/0033-295x.108.4.814

Haidt, J. (2003). The moral emotions. In R. J. Davidson, K. R. Scherer, & H. H. Goldsmith (Eds.), *Handbook of affective sciences* (Vol. 11, pp. 852–870). Oxford University Press.

References

Haidt, J. (2007). The new synthesis in moral psychology. *Science, 316*(5827), 998–1002. https://doi.org/10.1126/science.1137651

Hamlin, J. K., Wynn, K., Bloom, P., & Mahajan, N. (2011). How infants and toddlers react to antisocial others. *Proceedings of the National Academy of Sciences, 108*(50), 19931–19936. https://doi.org/10.1073/pnas.1110306108

Hamlin, J. Kiley, & Wynn, K. (2011). Young infants prefer prosocial to antisocial others. *Cognitive Development, 26*(1), 30–39. https://doi.org/10.1016/j.cogdev.2010.09.001

Hamlin, J. Kiley, Wynn, K., & Bloom, P. (2010). 3-month-olds show a negativity bias in their social evaluations. *Developmental Science, 13*(6), 923–929. https://doi.org/10.1111/j.1467-7687.2010.00951.x

Hasebe, Y., Nucci, L., & Nucci, M. (2004). Parental Control of the Personal Domain and Adolescent Symptoms of Psychopathology: A Cross-National Study in the United States and Japan. *Child Development, 75*, 815–828. https://doi.org/10.1111/j.1467-8624.2004.00708.x

Helwig, C. C. (1995). Adolescents' and young adults' conceptions of civil liberties: Freedom of speech and religion. *Child Development, 66*(1), 152–166. https://doi.org/10.2307/1131197

Helwig, C. C. (1995). Social context in social cognition: Psychological harm and civil liberties. In Melanie Killen & D. Hart (Eds.), *Morality in everyday life: Developmental perspectives* (pp. 166–200). Cambridge University Press.

Helwig, C. C. (1998). Children's conceptions of fair government and freedom of speech. *Child Development, 69*(2), 518–531. https://doi.org/10.2307/1132181

Helwig, C. C., Ruck, M. D., & Peterson-Badali, M. (2013). Rights, civil liberties, and democracy. In Melanie Killen & J. Smetana (Eds.), *Handbook of moral development,* (2nd ed., pp. 46–69). Psychology Press.

Henriques, G. (2008). Special section: The problem of psychology and the integration of human knowledge: contrasting

Wilson's consilience with the tree of knowledge system. *Theory & Psychology, 18*(6), 731–755. https://doi.org/10.1177/0959354308097255

Henriques, G. (2011). *A new unified theory of psychology.* Springer Science & Business Media.

Henriques, G. (2013). Evolving from methodological to conceptual unification. *Review of General Psychology, 17*(2), 168–173. https://doi.org/10.1037/a0032929

Hiser, J., & Koenigs, M. (2017). The multifaceted role of the ventromedial prefrontal cortex in emotion, decision making, social cognition, and psychopathology. *Biological Psychiatry, 83*(8), 638–647. https://doi.org/10.1016/j.biopsych.2017.10.030

Hoffman, M. (1970). Moral development. In P. H. Mussen (Ed.), *Carmichael's manual of child psychology* (Vol. 2, pp. 261–358). Wiley.

Hoffman, M. L. (2000). *Empathy and moral development: Implications for caring and justice.* Cambridge University Press.

Hoffman, M. L., & Saltzstein, H. D. (1967). Parent discipline and the child's moral development. *Journal of Personality and Social Psychology, 5*(1), 45–57. https://doi.org/10.1037/h0024189

How Do We Know Humans Are Primates? (2010, February 5). The Smithsonian Institution's Human Origins Program. http://humanorigins.si.edu/education/how-do-we-know/how-do-we-know-humans-are-primates

Hwang, J. Y. (2011). *Judgments of children and adolescents on exclusion and inclusion of a biracial peer in Korea.* University of California, Berkeley.

Hwang, J. Y. (2013). Judgments on exclusion of a biracial peer in Korea. *Theology and Philosophy, 23,* 213–254. https://doi.org/10.16936/theoph.23.23.201311.213

Izard, C. E. (1984). Emotion-cognition relationships and human development. In Carroll E. Izard, J. Kagan, & R. B. Zajonc

(Eds.), *Emotions, cognition, and behavior* (pp. 17–37). Cambridge University Press.

Izard, C. E. (1986). Approaches to developmental research on emotion-cognition relationships. In D. J. Bearison & H. Zimiles (Eds.), *Thought and emotion: developmental perspectives* (pp. 21–37). Erlbaum.

Jensen, K., & Silk, J. B. (2013). Searching for the evolutionary roots of human morality. In Melanie Killen & J. G. Smetana (Eds.), *Handbook of moral development* (2nd ed., pp. 475–494). Psychology Press.

Josi, S. H., Green, E. R., & Rogers, K. (2018). Biology. In *Encyclopedia Britannica*. Encyclopedia Britannica, inc. https://www.britannica.com/science/biology

JTBC News. (2020, April 15). *An interview with Yuval Noah Harari*. https://www.youtube.com/watch?v=15MwOw4l7NI&list=W L&index=4

Kahane, G. (2012). On the wrong track: Process and content in moral psychology. *Mind & Language, 27*(5), 519–545. https://doi.org/10.1111/mila.12001

Kahane, G. (2015). Sidetracked by trolleys: Why sacrificial moral dilemmas tell us little (or nothing) about utilitarian judgment. *Social Neuroscience, 10*(5), 551–560. https://doi.org/10.1080/17470919.2015.1023400

Kahane, G., Everett, J. A. C., Earp, B. D., Caviola, L., Faber, N. S., Crockett, M. J., & Savulescu, J. (2018). Beyond sacrificial harm: A two-dimensional model of utilitarian psychology. *Psychological Review, 125*(2), 131–164. https://doi.org/10.1037/rev0000093

Kahane, G., Everett, J. A. C., Earp, B. D., Farias, M., & Savulescu, J. (2015). 'Utilitarian' judgments in sacrificial moral dilemmas do not reflect impartial concern for the greater good. *Cognition, 134*, 193–209. https://doi.org/10.1016/j.cognition.2014.10.005

Kant, I. (1785). *Fundamental principles of the metaphysic of morals*. Liberal Arts Press.

Killen, M., & Smetana, J. (2007). The biology of morality: Human development and moral neuroscience. *Human Development, 50*, 241–243. https://doi.org/10.1159/000106413

Killen, M., & Smetana, J. (2008). Moral judgment and moral neuroscience: Intersections, definitions, and issues. *Child Development Perspectives, 2*(1), 1–6. https://doi.org/10.1111/j.1750-8606.2008.00033.x

Kim, J. M. (1998). Korean children's concepts of adult and peer authority and moral reasoning. *Developmental Psychology, 34*(5), 947–955. https://doi.org/10.1037/0012-1649.34.5.947

Kim, N. (2014). *The poetry of Kim Nam-ju.* Changbi.

Kochanska, G., Aksan, N., & Nichols, K. E. (2003). Maternal power assertion in discipline and moral discourse contexts: Commonalities, differences, and implications for children's moral conduct and cognition. *Developmental Psychology, 39*(6), 949–963. https://doi.org/10.1037/0012-1649.39.6.949

Koenigs, M., & Tranel, D. (2007). Irrational economic decision-making after ventromedial prefrontal damage: Evidence from the Ultimatum Game. *The Journal of Neuroscience, 27*(4), 951–956. https://doi.org/10.1523/JNEUROSCI.4606-06.2007

Koenigs, M., Kruepke, M., Zeier, J., & Newman, J. P. (2012). Utilitarian moral judgment in psychopathy. *Social Cognitive and Affective Neuroscience, 7*(6), 708–714. https://doi.org/10.1093/scan/nsr048

Koenigs, M., Young, L., Tranel, D., Cushman, F., Hauser, M., & Damasio, A. (2007). Damage to the prefrontal cortex increases utilitarian moral judgements. *Nature, 7138*(446), 908–911. https://doi.org/10.1038/nature05631

Kohlberg, L. (1968). The child as moral philosopher. *Psychology Today, 2*(4), 24–30.

Kohlberg, L. (1969). Stage and sequence: The cognitive development approach to socialization. In D. A. Goslin

(Ed.), *Handbook of socialization theory* (pp. 347–480). Rand McNally.

Kohlberg, L. (1970). Education for justice: A modern statement of the Platonic view. In N. F. Sizer & T. R. Sizer (Eds.), *Moral education: Five lectures* (pp. 57–83). Harvard University Press.

Kohlberg, L. (1971). From is to ought: How to commit the naturalistic fallacy and get away with it in the study of moral development. In T. Mischel (Ed.), *Cognitive development and epistemology* (pp. 151–232). Academic Press.

Kohlberg, L. (1981). *The philosophy of moral development: Moral stages and the idea of justice*. Harper & Row.

Kohlberg, L. (2008). The Development of children's orientations toward a moral order. *Human Development, 51*(1), 8–20. https://doi.org/10.1159/000112530

Koski, S., & Sterck, E. (2010). Empathic Chimpanzees: A proposal of the levels of emotional and cognitive processing in chimpanzee empathy. *European Journal of Developmental Psychology, 7,* 38–66. https://doi.org/10.1080/17405620902986991

Kramer, J., & Meunier, J. (2016). Kin and multilevel selection in social evolution: A never-ending controversy? *F1000Research, 5*(F 100 Faculty Rev):776, 1–13. https://doi.org/10.12688/f1000research.8018.1

Kuczynski, L., & Knafo, A. (2013). Innovation and continuity in socialization, internalization and acculturation. In M. Killen & A. Smetana (Eds.), *Handbook of moral development* (2nd ed., pp. 93–112). Psychology Press.

Kuhn, A. (2020, December 16). South Korea bans floating leaflets by balloon to North Korea. *NPR.Org.* https://www.npr.org/2020/12/16/947027288/south-korea-bans-floating-leaflets-by-balloon-to-north-korea

Lazarus, R. S. (1984). On the primacy of cognition. *American Psychologist, 39*(2), 124–129. https://doi.org/10.1037/0003-066X.39.2.124

References

Lazarus, R. S. (1991). *Emotion and adaptation.* Oxford University Press.

Lazarus, R. S. (1991). Cognition and motivation in emotion. *The American Psychologist, 46*(4), 352–367. https://doi.org/10.1037/0003-066X.46.4.352

Liszkowski, U., Carpenter, M., & Tomasello, M. (2008). Twelve-month-olds communicate helpfully and appropriately for knowledgeable and ignorant partners. *Cognition, 108*(3), 732–739. https://doi.org/10.1016/j.cognition.2008.06.013

Maienschein, J. (2017). Epigenesis and preformationism. In E. N. Zalta (Ed.), *The Stanford encyclopedia of philosophy* (Spring 2017 ed.). Metaphysics Research Lab, Stanford University. https://plato.stanford.edu/archives/spr2017/entries/epigenesis/

Malti, T., & Ongley, F. (2013). The development of moral emotions and moral reasoning. In Melanie Killen & J. Smetana (Eds.), *Handbook of moral development* (2nd ed., pp.163–183). Psychology Press.

Mandler, G. (1982). The structure of value: Accounting for taste. In M. S. Clark & S. T. Fiske (Eds.), *Affect and cognition* (pp. 3–36). Erlbaum.

McGuire, J., Langdon, R., Coltheart, M., & Mackenzie, C. (2009). A reanalysis of the personal/impersonal distinction in moral psychology research. *Journal of Experimental Social Psychology, 45*(3), 577–580. https://doi.org/10.1016/j.jesp.2009.01.002

Medicus, G. M. (1992). The inapplicability of the biogenetic rule to behavioral development. *Human Development, 35*(1), 1–8. https://doi.org/10.1159/000277108

Mencius. (2016). *Mencius: An online teaching translation* (R. Eno, Trans.). https://chinatxt.sitehost.iu.edu/Mencius%20(Eno-2016).pdf

Nichols, M. P., & Schwartz, R. C., coll. (2001). *The essentials of family therapy.* Allyn and Bacon.

References

Nieman, P., & Shea, S. (2004). Effective discipline for children. *Paediatrics & Child Health,*

9(1), 37–41. https://doi.org/10.1093/pch/9.1.37

Nowak, M. A., Tarnita, C. E., & Wilson, E. O. (2010). The evolution of eusociality. *Nature, 466*(7310), 1057–1062. https://doi.org/10.1038/nature09205

Nucci, L. P. (1981). Conceptions of personal issues: A domain distinct from moral or societal Concepts. *Child Development, 52*(1), 114–121. https://doi.org/10.2307/1129220

Nucci, L. P. (1996). Morality and the personal sphere of actions. In E. S. Reed, E. Turiel, & T. Brown (Eds.), *Values and knowledge* (pp. 41–60). Erlbaum.

Nucci, L. P. (2013). The personal and the moral. In Melanie Killen & J. G. Smetana (Eds.), *Handbook of moral development* (2nd ed., pp. 538–558). Psychology Press.

Nucci, L. P., & Smetana, J. G. (1996). Mothers' concepts of young children's areas of personal freedom. *Child Development, 67*(4), 1870–1886. https://doi.org/10.1111/j.1467-8624.1996.tb01833.x

Nucci, L. P., & Turiel, E. (1978). Social interactions and the development of social concepts in preschool children. *Child Development, 49*(2), 400–407. https://doi.org/10.2307/1128704

Nucci, L. P., & Turiel, E. (2009). Capturing the complexity of moral development and education. *Mind, Brain, and Education, 3*(3), 151–159. https://doi.org/10.1111/j.1751-228X.2009.01065.x

Nucci, L. P., & Weber, E. K. (1995). Social Interactions in the home and the development of young children's conceptions of the personal. *Child Development, 66*(5), 1438–1452. https://doi.org/10.2307/1131656

Nucci, L. P., Camino, C., & Sapiro, C. M. (1996). Social class effects on northeastern Brazilian children's conceptions of areas of personal choice and social regulation. *Child*

Development, 67(3), 1223-1242.
https://doi.org/10.1111/j.1467-8624.1996.tb01792.x

Nucci, L. P., Killen, M., & Smetana, J. G. (1996). Autonomy and the personal: Negotiation and social reciprocity in adult-child social exchanges. *New Directions for Child and Adolescent Development, 73,* 7-24.
https://doi.org/10.1002/cd.23219967303

Panksepp, J., Knutson, B., & Pruitt, D. L. (1988). Toward a neuroscience of emotion: The epigenetic foundation of emotional development. In M. F. Mascolo & S. Griffin (Eds.), *What develops in emotional development?* (pp. 53-84). Plenum Press.

Parks, R., & Haskins, J. (1999). *Rosa Parks: My story.* Puffin Books.

Piaget, J. (1929). *The child's conception of the world.* Routledge.

Piaget, J. (1932). *The moral judgment of the child.* Routledge.

Piaget, J. (1950). *The psychology of intelligence.* Routledge.

Piaget, J. (1952). *The origins of intelligence in children.* International Universities Press.

Piaget, J. (1954). *Intelligence and affectivity: Their relationship during child development.* Annual Reviews.

Piaget, J. (1965). *Sociological studies.* Routledge.

Piaget, J. (1966). Moral feelings and judgment. In H. E. Gruber & Voneche (Eds.), *The essential Piaget: An interpretive reference and guide* (pp. 154-158). Basic Books.

Piaget, J. (1971). *Biology and knowledge: An essay on the relations between organic regulations and cognitive processes.* University of Chicago Press.

Piaget, J., & Inhelder, B. (1969). *The psychology of the child.* Basic Books.

Pinker, S. (2015). The false allure of group selection. In D. M. Buss (Ed.), *The handbook of evolutionary psychology* (pp. 1-14). John Wiley & Sons.

Rakoczy, H., Warneken, F., & Tomasello, M. (2008). The sources of normativity: Young children's awareness of the normative structure of games. *Developmental Psychology, 44*(3), 875–881. https://doi.org/10.1037/0012-1649.44.3.875

Rawls, J. (1971). *A theory of justice.* Harvard University Press.

Rosa Parks. (2020). In *Wikipedia.* https://en.wikipedia.org/w/index.php?title=Rosa_Parks&oldid=962525099

Rosas, A., & Koenigs, M. (2014). Beyond "utilitarianism": Maximizing the clinical impact of moral judgment research. *Social Neuroscience, 9*(6), 661–667. https://doi.org/10.1080/17470919.2014.937506

Schaffer, H. R. (2006). *Key concepts in developmental psychology.* Sage.

Sen, A. (1985). Well-being, agency and freedom: The Dewey lectures 1984. *The Journal of Philosophy, 82*(4), 169–221. https://doi.org/10.2307/2026184

Sen, A. (2006). Reason, freedom and well-being. *Utilitas, 18*(1), 80–96. https://doi.org/10.1017/S0953820805001846

Seyfarth, R., & Cheney, D. (1984). Grooming alliances and reciprocal altruism in vervet monkeys. *Nature, 308,* 541–543. https://doi.org/10.1038/308541a0

Skinner, B. F. (1974). *About behaviorism.* Vintage Books.

Skinner, B. F. (1978). *Reflections on behaviorism and society.* Prentice Hall.

Skinner, B. F. (1981). Selection by consequences. *Science, 213*(4507), 501–504. https://doi.org/10.1126/science.7244649

Skinner, B. F. (2013). *Contingencies of reinforcement: A theoretical analysis.* B. F. Skinner Foundation.

Smetana, J. (1981a). Reasoning in the personal and moral domains: Adolescent and young adult women's decision-making regarding abortion. *Journal of Applied Developmental Psychology, 2*(3), 211–226. https://doi.org/10.1016/0193-3973(81)90002-2

Smetana, J. (1981b). Preschool children's conceptions of moral and social rules. *Child Development,* 1333–1336. https://doi.org/10.2307/1129527

Smetana, J. (1983). Social-cognitive development: Domain distinctions and coordinations. *Developmental Review, 3*(2), 131–147. https://doi.org/10.1016/0273-2297(83)90027-8

Smetana, J. (1999). The role of parents in moral development: A social domain analysis. *Journal of Moral Education, 28,* 311–321. https://doi.org/10.1080/030572499103106

Smetana, J. (2006). Social-cognitive domain theory: Consistency and variations in children's moral and social judgements. In M. Killen & J. Smetana (Eds.), *Handbook of moral development* (pp. 119–153). Lawrence Erlbaum.

Snyder, C. (2016, March 30). *Freedom and discipline.* Baan Dek. https://baandek.org/posts/freedom-discipline/

Steinberg, L., & Monahan, K. C. (2007). Age differences in resistance to peer influence. *Developmental Psychology, 43*(6), 1531–1543. https://doi.org/10.1037/0012-1649.43.6.1531

Talmi, D., & Frith, C. (2007). Neurobiology: Feeling right about doing right. *Nature, 446,* 865–866. https://doi.org/10.1038/446865a

Tomasello, M. (2014). The ultra-social animal. *European Journal of Social Psychology, 44*(3), 187–194. https://doi.org/10.1002/ejsp.2015

Tomasello, M., Melis, A. P., Tennie, C., Wyman, E., & Herrmann, E. (2012). Two key steps in the evolution of human cooperation: The interdependence hypothesis. *Current Anthropology, 53*(6), 673–692. https://doi.org/10.1086/668207

Tomlinson, S. (2011, November 22). *Schoolboy who wore skirt to class in row over uniform rules is awarded prestigious human rights prize.* Mail Online. https://www.dailymail.co.uk/news/article-2064924/Chris-Whitehead-skirt-Schoolboy-13-awarded-prestigious-human-rights-prize.html

References

Turiel, E. (1977). Distinct conceptual and developmental domains: Social convention and morality. *Nebraska Symposium on Motivation.* http://psycnet.apa.org/psycinfo/1980-22343-001

Turiel, E. (1983). *The development of social knowledge: Morality and convention.* Cambridge University Press.

Turiel, E. (2002). *The culture of morality: Social development, context, and conflict.* Cambridge University Press.

Turiel, E. (2006a). The development of morality. In W. Damon & N. Eisenberg (Eds.), *Handbook of child psychology: Social, emotional and personality development* (Vol. 3, pp. 789–857). Wiley.

Turiel, E. (2006b). Thought, emotions, social interactional processes in moral development. In M. Killen & J. Smetana (Eds.), *Handbook of moral development* (pp. 7–35). Erlbaum.

Turiel, E. (2007). Social decisions, social interactions, and the coordination of diverse judgments. In U. Mueller, J. I. Carpendale, N. Budwig, & B. Sokol (Eds.), *Social life, social knowledge: Toward a process account of development* (pp. 255–276). Erlbaum.

Turiel, E, & Wainryb, C. (1998). Concepts of freedoms and rights in a traditional, hierarchically organized society. *British Journal of Developmental Psychology, 16*(3), 375–395. https://doi.org/10.1111/j.2044-835X.1998.tb00759.x

UNICEF. (n.d.). *The Convention on the Rights of the Child: The children's version.* Retrieved February 12, 2021, from https://www.unicef.org/child-rights-convention/convention-text-childrens-version

Universal Declaration of Human Rights. (1948). https://www.un.org/en/universal-declaration-human-rights/

Vaish, A., & Tomasello, M. (2013). The early ontogeny of human cooperation and morality. In Melanie Killen & J. G. Smetana (Eds.), *Handbook of moral development* (2nd ed., pp. 279–298). Psychology Press.

References

Warneken, F., Chen, F., & Tomasello, M. (2006). Cooperative activities in young children and chimpanzees. *Child Development, 77*(3), 640–663. https://doi.org/10.1111/j.1467-8624.2006.00895.x

Wessel, A. (2009). What is epigenesis? Or Gene's place in development. *Human Ontogenetics, 3*(2), 35–37. https://doi.org/10.1002/huon.200900008

West, S. A., Griffin, A. S., & Gardner, A. (2007). Social semantics: Altruism, cooperation, mutualism, strong reciprocity and group selection. *Journal of Evolutionary Biology, 20*(2), 415–432. https://doi.org/10.1111/j.1420-9101.2006.01258.x

Weston, D. R., & Turiel, E. (1980). Act-rule relations: Children's concepts of social rules. *Developmental Psychology, 16*(5), 417–424. https://doi.org/10.1037/0012-1649.16.5.417

Williams, G. (2018). Kant's account of reason. In E. N. Zalta (Ed.), *The Stanford encyclopedia of philosophy* (Summer 2018). Metaphysics Research Lab, Stanford University. https://plato.stanford.edu/archives/sum2018/entries/kant-reason/

Wilson, D. S., & Dugatkin, L. A. (1997). Group selection and assortative interactions. *The American Naturalist, 149*(2), 336–351. https://doi.org/10.1086/285993

Wilson, D. S., & Sober, E. (1994). Reintroducing group selection to the human behavioral sciences. *Behavioral and Brain Sciences, 17*(4), 585–608. https://doi.org/10.1017/s0140525x00036104

Wilson, D. S., & Wilson, E. O. (2007). Rethinking the theoretical foundation of sociobiology. *The Quarterly Review of Biology, 82*(4), 327–348. https://doi.org/10.1086/522809

Wilson, E. O. (1975). *Sociobiology: The new synthesis.* Belknap Press.

Wilson, E. O. (1978). *On human nature.* Harvard University Press.

Wilson, E. O. (2005). Kin selection as the key to altruism: Its rise and fall. *Social Research, 72*(1), 159–166. https://www.jstor.org/stable/40972006

References

Wilson, E. O. (2012). *The social conquest of earth*. WW Norton & Co.

Wilson, E. O., & Hölldobler, B. (2005). Eusociality: Origin and consequences. *Proceedings of the National Academy of Sciences, 102*(38), 13367–13371. https://doi.org/10.1073/pnas.0505858102

Wynn, K., & Bloom, P. (2013). The moral baby. In Melanie Killen & J. G. Smetana (Eds.), *Handbook of moral development* (2nd ed., pp. 435–453). Psychology Press. https://doi.org/10.4324/9780203581957

Wynn, K., Bloom, P., Jordan, A., Marshall, J., & Sheskin, M. (2018). Not noble savages after all: Limits to early altruism. *Current Directions in Psychological Science, 27*(1), 3–8. https://doi.org/10.1177/0963721417734875

Xunzi. (2014). *Xunzi: The complete text* (E. L. Hutton, Trans.). Princeton University Press.

Zajonc, R. B. (1984). On the primacy of affect. *American Psychologist, 39*(2), 117–123. https://doi.org/10.1037/0003-066X.39.2.117

Zhang, Q. (2016). *Human dignity in Classical Chinese philosophy: Confucianism, Mohism, and Daoism*. Palgrave Macmillan.

Zimmerman, M. J., & Bradley, B. (2019). Intrinsic vs. Extrinsic Value. In E. N. Zalta (Ed.), *The Stanford encyclopedia of philosophy* (Spring 2019 ed.). Metaphysics Research Lab, Stanford University. https://plato.stanford.edu/archives/spr2019/entries/value-intrinsic-extrinsic/

N